A GUIDE TO TAROT AND Relationships

A GUIDE TO TAROT AND Relationships

Andria K. Molina

ARTWORK BY DOLORES FITCHIE

Schiffer Publishing Ltd
4880 Lower Valley Road • Atglen, PA 19310

Copyright © 2012 by Andria K. Molina

Text by Andria K. Molina
Artwork by Delores Fitchie

Library of Congress Control Number: 2012947800

All rights reserved. No part of this work may be reproduced or used in any form or by any means – graphic, electronic, or mechanical, including photocopying or information storage and retrieval systems – without written permission from the publisher.

The scanning, uploading and distribution of this book or any part thereof via the Internet or via any other means without the permission of the publisher is illegal and punishable by law. Please purchase only authorized editions and do not participate in or encourage the electronic piracy of copyrighted materials.

"Schiffer," "Schiffer Publishing, Ltd. & Design," and the "Design of pen and inkwell" are registered trademarks of Schiffer Publishing, Ltd.

Designed by Danielle D. Farmer
Type set in Fiolex Girls/Futura XBlk BT/Avenir LT Std

ISBN: 978-0-7643-4232-5
Printed in The United States

Schiffer Books are available at special discounts for bulk purchases for sales promotions or premiums. Special editions, including personalized covers, corporate imprints, and excerpts can be created in large quantities for special needs. For more information contact the publisher:

Published by Schiffer Publishing, Ltd.
4880 Lower Valley Road
Atglen, PA 19310
Phone: (610) 593-1777; Fax: (610) 593-2002
E-mail: Info@schifferbooks.com

For the largest selection of fine reference books on this and related subjects, please visit our website at **www.schifferbooks.com**
We are always looking for people to write books on new and related subjects. If you have an idea for a book, please contact us at **proposals@schifferbooks.com**

This book may be purchased from the publisher.
Please try your bookstore first.
You may write for a free catalog.

In Europe, Schiffer books are distributed by
Bushwood Books
6 Marksbury Ave.
Kew Gardens
Surrey TW9 4JF England
Phone: 44 (0) 20 8392 8585; Fax: 44 (0) 20 8392 9876
E-mail: info@bushwoodbooks.co.uk
Website: www.bushwoodbooks.co.uk

DEDICATION

To my grandmother, Kay Alba, for her intriguing Tarot stories; my great-grandmother, Melchora Valdes Rangel, a mystic Tarot reader; my sister, Sonya, for directing me to Schiffer Publishing; my supportive and encouraging parents, Joe and Bertha; and my loving husband, Dr. Suleiman. Also to my friend Aaron and the Tarot community.

ACKNOWLEDGMENTS

I would like to thank Dolores Fitchie for her contribution in allowing me to use her artistic work of her *Gorgon Tarot* deck that adds visual decadence to the book. Also, Dinah Roseberry for her expertise in polishing my script and Schiffer Publishing in accepting my proposal, bringing my creative idea into existence.

CONTENTS

8   Preface

9   **CHAPTER 1**   Introduction
                                  Relationship Questions and Examples of Spreads
                                  Tips On Working with the Tarot
                                  Symbolism
                                  How to Use This Book

19   **CHAPTER 2**   The Major Arcane

59   **CHAPTER 3**   The Seasonal Arcane

67   **CHAPTER 4**   The Pip Cards

127   **CHAPTER 5**   The Royalty Cards

143   **CHAPTER 6**   Court of the Knights

151   **CHAPTER 7**   Court of the Pages

159   Conclusion

PREFACE

The purpose of this book is to take the consciousness and its exploration to a deeper level through the understanding of your relationships using the metaphorical language of Tarot. Some may ask: Why read this book? What makes this book any different from other Tarot books? This book was made especially for one to gain insight into what dialogue is being presented in a relationship. Tarot has the natural ability to enhance one's intuitive awareness, and with that, one can capture the needed assessment in any situation.

Chapter 1
Introduction

Now it's time to gain some insight into relationships! There are many aspects to a relationship, whether it's birth order, childhood upbringing, or astrological signs – it's multifactorial. When using this book as a guide, try to see how the information presented here relates to *your* relationships. Tarot is a unique tool that can give clarity into any question asked. The usage of Tarot helps the reader to have a better understanding of a situation or circumstance. A question I often like to address involves people asking me to tell them winning lottery numbers. They ask me: If someone is psychic, then shouldn't they know the numbers? Tarot readings aren't meant for that kind of gratification; the Tarot is meant to work with a person's personal growth.

RELATIONSHIP QUESTIONS AND EXAMPLES OF SPREADS

Soulmate Spread: *Is he or she my Soulmate?*

I have found as a Tarot reader that the word *soulmate* is not limited. A lot of people have asked me during their readings: Is he or she my soulmate? This is a great question; many view the meaning of soulmate as the ultimate one who they will spend their life with. However, a soulmate can come in many forms. For example, we can have a soulmate for a book club, one for exercising, or even someone to work with in metaphysical studies. This is something that we share with that person with deep affinity making the relationship unique and the connection fully bonded while learning from each other in symbiotic give and take.

I have found this type of spread useful in clarifying the question of soulmate.

Card 1: What type of friendship/partner is this? (Bottom Card)

Card 2: What is the friendship's/partner's intention? (Top Card)

Card 3: What lesson will I learn from them? (Left Side Card)

Card 4: What lesson will they learn from me? (Right Side Card)

Card 5: The Progression of the unionship. (Middle of the spread)

The Ratio 1:1 Spread: *Stay or Leave?*

This question comes up often. For example, Tina, a 26-year-old banker wanted to know if Craig was going to leave his current fiancé to be with her. Tina and Craig worked together and had been seeing each other. Tina had given him an ultimatum the week prior to her reading. The Tarot spread went as follows:

Card 1: Stay with me?
Card drawn: Empress

Card 2: Leave Current Partner?
Card drawn: 6 of Swords

Time Frame: *One-Card Spread*

Card 1: Weekly, Monthly, Years
Card drawn: 5 of Wands

Interpretation:

My interpretation was: Yes, Craig would leave his current fiancé. The Empress is a strong *yes* card and also, for me, it depicted that Craig saw Tina as a wife of his desire. 6 of Swords was an indicator of movement away from the current partner, with a time frame of 5 weeks. In doing Tarot readings, the cards have multiple interpretations – this is where your skills comes in as a reader. For example, in the above situation, one can say that the Empress could have meant that Craig saw Tina just as a girlfriend and 6 of swords tells us that Craig's relationship with his fiancé was moving in a better direction.

Will He or She Propose to Me?

This is a one-card spread followed by the Zodiac spread. In the Zodiac spread, lay out 12 cards, one for each month of the year. Shuffle the full card deck and place each card next to one another. From there, you can determine what patterns will most likely occur in that particular month.

Some cards that I have experienced as high energy cards for marriage proposals are the Knights, Ace of Swords, 8 of Cups, 9 of Cups, 9 of Pentacles, and 10 of Wands.

Example

Beverly, a 45-year-old mother and realtor from Hawaii, was anxious to get married and start a new life with her current boyfriend, Bob. She had been dating Bob for one year and wanted to know when was Bob going to propose to her, and where?

This is a two-part question.

Card 1: One card for a *yes* or *no* followed by Zodiac Spread

1-Card Spread: *What is he or she thinking of me?*

I get this question a lot when the client's relationship is relatively new, or a major event/crises had taken place in the relationship. When a client seeks this type of question, you will find that the Tarot mirrors back or reflects how they feel about themselves in a partial or deep-seeded way. This is a way to see the other person's conscious thinking of the client. I always use a 1-Card Spread for this; I find it to be the most effective way for me to provide an answer.

For example, Samantha, a 27-year-old graduate student called me for a reading regarding a new guy she'd met at a friend's party. She was excited and hopeful in the possibilities surrounding him. Her first question was: "What does Kenny think of me?" I immediately resorted to the 1-Card Spread. Her reading went as follows:

Card 1: One card for the answer
Card drawn: Ace of Wands

Interpretation:

It appeared that Kenny was excited about the beginning with Samantha, viewing her as a strong, sharp, intellectual women. Physically, he viewed her as an elegant dresser with well-kept hair and makeup. In relation to communication, Kenny found Samantha to be an idealist. She had her own rules about how a relationship should be or what a boyfriend should do for her (like opening the car door and paying for the dates). Also, she was seen as ambitious and loved to be the center of attention. She liked compliments.

TIPS ON WORKING WITH THE TAROT

Picking a Deck

When working with the Tarot over the years, I have found that it's important to pick a deck that you can relate to and read with. Some decks are really pretty and colorful, but when you open them up and actually do readings with them, you may find that they're not as easy flowing when reading with them. If you have a particular deck that you're interested in, you can go online and take a look at the imagery to see if the deck is something you can work with. If you're a beginner, it may be helpful to pick a deck that has a general meaning on each card; from there you can work your way up from the meaning to add to your own interpretation.

Reading

Reading Tarot can be fun and unique. I find that the Tarot offers a metaphorical view into someone's situation, and a Tarot reading can give clarity or a different insight into a question. It's useful to refrain from your own personal view, comments, or judgments as you take this view, however; just read what you see in the cards. From time to time, I've come across readers who add their opinions to readings. This isn't effective, because the client isn't interested in personal views or opinions. The reading is theirs alone. I find that when a reader adds opinions, it actually inhibits the reading and the level of accuracy diminishes.

For example, Sophia, a 28-year-old Catholic medical student, wanted to fly to South Africa to meet her Muslim mother-in-law for the first time. Her mother-in-law was there for some medical testing and her husband had already flown in. So Sophia had consulted a Tarot reading to see how it would go if she, too, flew to South Africa.

The first thing the reader heard was that the person she was reading for was Catholic and her mother-in-law was Muslim. The reader began to talk about how backwards she felt religions were and how things would never work out. She was imparting information that she'd gleaned from her neighbor, instead of just reading the Tarot for the woman in front of her. The reader was giving her judgments and opinions.

It so happens that Sophia had a very favorable outcome in her trip and is in a great relationship with her mother in-law.

You will find that as you enhance your intuitive ability, and the more readings you conduct, the stronger your ability will be to pick up different things. Just leave opinions out!

Preparing for Readings

Like anything else, the more you do something, the better you become. Enhancing or developing your intuition is an added benefit in reading Tarot. There are a multiple of ways to do this – for instance, meditate for 15 to 30 minutes a day. Not only does meditation help reduce your body's stress level (from hormones like cortisol), it helps you stay connected to your mind and body. Listening to self hypnosis CDs before going to sleep is another way to increase the level of intuition. Yoga is a great way to bring flexibility to the body; obtaining this is a great way to keep the body healthy. Try to make all of these, or one of these, a habit in your daily lifestyle.

Also, keep a journal of your readings. Write down important points that come up when you read for your clients. (When you have repeat clients, they will follow up with you from prior readings, and having a journal will allow you to learn more about those readings and can help you understand where – if at all – your interpretation was off.) Later, in future readings, your past experiences can help increase your accuracy.

Hypnosis also allows one to reach the Theta state, which is part of the brain wave levels. This brain level is great for mediumship/psychic/Tarot work; also, it's naturally heightened in children below the age of 10 years of age. Have you ever wondered why you hear children say they see an imaginary friend or you yourself were psychic around that age? Well, that's because being in the Theta state allows you to "work" in that level, naturally enhancing your psyche.

Using incense, aromatherapy, and sageing is a great way to clear the energy in your reading work space. I also found that incorporating Reiki in clearing the Chakra centers opens up a clear, flowing energy and helps in creative Tarot readings.

SYMBOLISM

General Information on Chakras

Throughout our bodies, we have energy systems that are located in the major organs of the human anatomy referred to as Chakras. Each Chakra has its own distinctive number, color, and key meaning that relates to the human psyche, which begins to formulate at the beginning of the behavioral nurturing process and nature's development. The Chakra is a Sanskrit word that has the meaning *the coiled one*, and each coiled one has its own name (referred to by the 7 names that are listed below). Chakras intertwine in a Tarot reading and can aid in insightful development. The significance of each Chakra follows:

- 1st **Chakra**, which is referred to as Muludhara, governs the base of the spine; key issues with security and survival; color association red.
- 2nd **Chakra**, which is referred to as Swadhisthaanna, governs the groin; key issues with sexuality, creativity, and relationships; color association orange.
- 3rd **Chakra**, which is referred to as Manipura, governs the Solar Plexus, abdominal area; key issues with self esteem, confidence, and opinions; color association yellow.
- 4th **Chakra**, which is referred to as Anahata, governs the heart; key issues conditional/unconditional love, codependency, and self care; color association is green or pink.
- 5th **Chakra**, which is referred to as Vishuddha, governs the throat; key issues communication, self expression, and suppression of thought; color association is blue.
- 6th **Chakra**, which is referred to as Ajna, governs the 3rd eye; key issues awareness, intuition, and relaxation; color association can be dark blue, white and indigo.
- 7th **Chakra**, which is referred to as Sahasrara, governs the Crown; key issue consciousness and being in the presence; color association violet.

General Information on Numerology

When reading Tarot, there may be times when the spread depicts several cards of the same number; for instance, you may notice that there are several 8 in the spread. Eights are associated with change, so the spread is indicating that there is significant change relating to that area of the spread and that particular suite that the eights represents.

Each Tarot card has its own number; this is a general theme of each number:

Ones: Start and Beginnings
Twos: Duality
Threes: Building
Fours: Maintaining
Fives: Work Together
Sixes: Success with Change
Sevens: Prosperity
Eights: Change
Nines: Independence
Tens: Responsibility

General Information on Elements

Wands: Wood, Fire
Cups: Water, Emotions
Swords: Air, Metal
Pentacles: Earth, Ground

HOW TO USE THIS BOOK

The beginning section detailing each card contains information about the planet, ruling sign, and Chakras as well as Tarot card meanings; the second section goes into depth about relationships. You may find that some information pertains to your reading and some does not – this is to be expected. I am sometimes asked: How do I know what relates to me in the reading? This is where your intuition will guide you. To be an effective reader, it takes knowledge of the Tarot as well as being intuitive. The metaphorical section for each card was designed to give you the *feeling* of the card, and the general meanings section relates to any question that is asked. The question statement is to make you think in an analytical way, and the affirmation is to create positive thinking. The timing part can give a frame or period.

The more you study different meanings in the cards and heighten your intuition, the easier readings become.

Chapter 2
The Major Arcane

The Fool
THE UNKNOWN JOURNEY

Planet: Uranus – brings unexpected, independent, rebellious

Ruled by Aquarius: Fixed, *I know*

1st Chakra: The Base – Wanting, color red

Location: 4th sacral vertebrae (tail bone)

Fool in a relationship can depict someone who has never experienced this type of relationship or situation before. So, the feelings one may be experiencing are anxiety or fear because this new kind of pairing brings the unfamiliar into one's life. There may be emotional fear out of distrust of the unknown and what will develop in the relationship. This can create doubt in entering or staying in the relationship and what actions should be carried out.

Developing self-awareness of one's strong and weak points, or beliefs and intentions, can create healthy self-esteem that can eliminate the fear in entering the relationship, or for it to continue. This can be an exciting time and completely open and free of any controlling situations. Learning more about one's partner and what they want out of the relationship or life can alleviate some sense of fear and give the one in question more comfort in taking the unknown journey with their partner.

There is an open mind for each partner in this relationship; both are willing to try different approaches that expose them to new things or ideas. Going into the relationship with self-liberation, freedom, and independence from any past hindrances awakens unconventional ideas. This will bring new thoughts and creativity into the relationship, but also some chaos.

Your partner may be friends with all different types of people and cultures. An unexpected event is a positive learning tool for life and love relationships.

Metaphorical

This relationship is like traveling to a new country where you've not been before, and never experiencing the actions and events that took place to get to the new location. Faith and excitement leads to a path of new experiences.

GENERAL MEANING FOR THE FOOL

- Unexpected events, stable and secure time to make a move in a career or relationship
- Moving over water or near water, spontaneous, revolution, innocence, trusting of your inner voice
- Travel to a new country
- Trusting faith, moving through, blinded by the unknown
- Being led through divine design
- Being taken advantage of, lack of discipline from the inability to take responsibility, naïve, moving forward in career plans in a new direction, using your back-up plan
- New job, career, being accepted for a financial loan, or academic school acceptance

Question statement:
What's one thing that brings you fear in your relationship?

Affirmation:
Self-awareness allows me to pay attention to the details of
my emotions and behavior.

Time frame:
1 Week, 22 days, January 21-February 18

The Magician
JACK AND THE BOX

Planet: Mercury – Communication, reasoning and thinking ability

Ruled by earth sign Virgo and air sign Gemini: Virgo – Mutable, *I analyze*; Gemini – Mutable, *I think*

2nd Chakra: Sacral – Desire, color orange

Location: Lumbar region, 1st vertebra

The Magician is about controlling issues, learning to accept and reject. There are 4 symbols:

1. A sword, which represents effective communication, speaking in the relationship, listening to one's partner – without interruption
2. A wand, which can mean core beliefs, reasoning in the relationship, not judging a partner for what they believe in
3. A pentacle, which can represent stability in the relationship, allowing partners to learn from each other
4. A cup, which represents the emotions and how one reasons with angry, fearful, happy, and sad moments in the relationship

The Magician is a very positive card having the 4 elements, earth (pentacles), air (swords), fire (wands), and water (cups), which means that the relationship, or the partner being asked about, has all the key ingredients to make it work and move forward.

The relationship is in a good place; communication is being practiced on both sides by listening to one another and allowing a better understanding of each other. Partners can relate to each other when talking, and can share or respect each other's core beliefs.

Financially, both are stable and emotionally meeting each other's needs.

On the flip side, one of the partners may be missing one, or all, of the key elements in the relationship. Someone may have a difficult time in communicating their feelings, or have different core beliefs. The stability may not be there, or there may be a lot of emotional issues from the past that hinder the relationship.

When this occurs, someone may be staying in the relationship in hopes that it will change. For example, let's say that one is dating or has married a partner who grew up believing that it was their partner's job to "do the dishes." Or, maybe a partner doesn't want to have children and this is ingrained in core beliefs. The thinking may be that his or her own core belief will change with time, only later to find out that it doesn't change. So, there is an influence of illusion that this relationship will work, and tricking oneself out of the real truth just to stay in the relationship is a negative action. Tricking one's self out of emotions only abandons true needs.

METAPHORICAL

This relationship is like the candy bar that has all the tasty ingredients: chocolate (cups), almonds (pentacles), caramel (cups), and wafer (wands). But if you remove one of those elements, it may still taste good, but the feeling something is missing is there. The candy will not taste the same. This is true for any kind of relationship as well.

GENERAL MEANING FOR THE MAGICIAN

- Trickery, control, sleight of hand that leads to falseness
- Illusion, confidence, improved career, finances, and health, seizing opportunity
- Fraud, sharp tongue, soulmate "momentary," unexpected love interest
- Hoax, strong personality, manipulation that leads to abuse of authority
- Swindle, skillful, collaboration, or support

Question statement:
What 4 elements do you share with your partner?

Affirmation:
I communicate supportive and healthy words; I honor my belief system, I'm thankful for my financial position and I'm emotionally supportive to all around me.

Timing:
1 Week 3rd Day, or Wednesday; 5th month, 8th month or 9th month;
May 21-June 21, August 23-September 22

The High Priestess
UNIQUE INTUITIVE WOMEN

Moon: Instinct, emotions, subconscious

Ruled by water sign Cancer: Cardinal, I feel

3rd Chakra: Solar plexus, color yellow

Location: Thoracic vertebrae 7th, 8th, behind the stomach

In a relationship spread, this card can mean that there is a women figure around the couple who has an influence on their relationship – this can be good or bad. The person adding their comments to the relationship can be a judgmental individual, or an emotional manipulator. Just remember, it's the two people *in* the relationship that matter and know what really goes on between each partner. This card represents the unconscious, which is the back-seat driver to one's thoughts. Since the partners already know what or where the relationship is headed, the added input from another person is not needed.

Personal feelings regarding how one feels with their partner may show a sense of being powerless or powerful. Both are sensitive to each other's words and actions. What is needed and wanted in the relationship is important to nurture the needs for both partners.

On the flip side, one in the partnership may be over sensitive with emotions and this could cause an overreaction of fits and anger, making one partner feel that they need to adjust their own emotional interactions with that partner. Overly emotional reactions can be idiopathic (spurred by an unknown cause), or from side effects of birth control pills, or childhood suppression of emotions. This can lead to superficial sex, with no relationship.

Pay attention to dreams and psychic impressions. Learn more about one's Inner Self and how one can react to the actions of their partner and how to govern emotions and beliefs in the relationship.

Metaphorical

You're lost and on the road. Your own intuition is telling you to turn left to get to your destination; then the person with you tells you: "No, turn right." Who are you going to listen to?

GENERAL MEANING FOR THE HIGH PRIESTESS

- Girlfriend, intuition, listen to your inner voice, exposing a lie or secret
- Manipulation, extramarital affair, success in the work place, finances
- Platonic friend, education, fertility, virginity

Question Statement:
Who has an outside influence regarding your relationship? Is it positive or negative?

Affirmation:
I make positive decisions in my relationship.

Timing:
1 week, 1 lunar cycle, 1st of the month, Monday, summer, June 21-July 22

NATURE VERSUS NURTURER

Planet: Venus – Sensual, love

Ruled by earth sign Taurus and air sign Libra: Taurus – Fixed, *I build;* Libra – Cardinal, *I balance*

4th Chakra: To give and receive love, colors green or pink

Location: Heart, thoracic vertebrae

The Empress depicts a growing time in your relationship, partners feeling "apple of the eye" sentiments. The growing or gestation period in the relationship can mean that both partners are working on different or same projects, like family goals, such as career, work, or house-related topics. This is a positive *yes* card, so if one is waiting for a certain *yes* or *no* answer to a dilemma, that response will most likely be *yes*.

In a relationship, the Empress relates to the nurturer, so one of the partners may be the nurturer who is supportive or adds new ideas to the relationship. Or one may be feeling that the relationship lacks the nurturing, that a lot of effort is put forth but lacks reciprocal support from the other partner. Vulnerability to stress triggers may be indicated, due to the lack of nurturing that is needed in the relationship.

Also, one partner may have a tendency to keep their real emotions to themselves. Take a look at the surrounding environment and how it has an influence on the relationship; this can be a positive or negative support. The focus could be on how the household is run, if there is equal input into the home environment. One partner may spend more in the relationship, whereas the other is a saver. Due to social cultural and family upbringing, one may have grown up not expressing affection. Both partners enjoy the sensual pleasures of the relationship but one partner would like more nurturing because of this. Being open and vulnerable in a relationship is important. There may be a need to interact more with friends; this can eliminate any restriction or loneliness one may be feeling in the relationship. One may be very emotional and easy to react in a conversation because, unconsciously, they are not getting the nurturing support needed.

Metaphorical

When one buys fruit at the market – like apples – he or she washes them at home with water (nature) to rinse off the impurities, then polish (nurture) before taking a bite, and finally, the sensual pleasure of the fruit is enjoyed. Nature and Nurture go hand in hand in growth.

GENERAL MEANING FOR THE EMPRESS

- Wife, success, which can lead to many things opening up, inspirational
- Girlfriend, miscarriage/infertile, indecisions
- Pregnancy/fertility, ignorance that leads to hidden actions
- Beauty, anxiety, comfortable living
- Enjoying Self Care for ones personal growth

Question statement:
In your relationship, is the more supportive partner you or your partner, and is it reciprocal back to you or your partner?

Affirmation:
I'm grateful for all the love and beauty that surrounds my relationship each day.

Time Frame:
1 week, or 9 months, 5th day, May 20-June 20, September 23-October 23

The Emperor
TAKING CONTROL

Planet: Mars – Taking action, temper

Ruled by fire sign Aries: Cardinal, *I am*

5th Chakra: Throat; color blue

Location: 3rd cervical vertebra, bottom of the neck

    The Emperor card can represent corrective actions that take place in a relationship. This can be a positive card; things from the past that needed to be addressed and dealt with are now being handled and have a positive outcome.

    Also indicated is the possibility of a partner who has a controlling personality; the Emperor represents Aries in astrology, and this may depict one of the partner's traits. One partner may see the correct actions needing to be taken in the relationship, being the mind of reasoning and strength combined to make the decisions. One may feel like their partner has to prove something (or themselves) about how they behave or if the relationship is worthy. Someone who is wise and has a mindset older than their age may be indicated and this is reflected by their actions. A partner may have a hot temper; one may be quick to argue and question motives (driven by their suspicious personality). Expressiveness is a need to be expressed in a relationship, what is wanted out of the partnering, what direction each individual wants to explore, and where it is headed.

    Is the communication two-way? When both are talking, who is on the receiving end of the conversation? With strong personalities, it can be difficult to hear both sides of the conversation because no one is listening to what the other partner is saying. They often focus on getting their own point of view heard rather than resolving problems, so the issue at hand never gets addressed. This fuels anger and frustration. Get to the point where both sides are heard without interrupting or walking away. Listen and wait 10 seconds before responding to the partner's point of view, and vice versa. This will allow both individuals to speak without having one partner doing all the talking and the other just sitting and listening. Masculine energy and dogmatic rules can influence or play a role in the relationship.

Metaphorical

A Boxer Porsche is a popular car for women, and eye catching for men. The strength and dominance naturally commands respect on the highway (and in a relationship).

GENERAL MEANING FOR EMPEROR

- Control, competition, good business mind
- Independent, rebellion against rules, leadership qualities
- Loves challenges, easily irritated, black mail/manipulator
- Good judgment, success, thoughtfulness
- Strong minded, goal oriented, business proposal being accepted

Question Statement:
What is one thing that you're dealing with in your relationship that has taken time? Are the conversations between you and your partner open ended with both listening and communicating views?

Affirmation:
I enjoy sharing and I listen to my partner.

Timing:
1 week, 4 months, March 21-April 19

This card represents the hierarchy of religion. In relationships, it indicates the

#

CORE BELIEFS

Planet: Venus – Sensual desires

Ruled by earth sign Taurus: Fixed, *I build*

3rd Chakra: Desire for happiness, color yellow

Location: Solar plexus

beliefs that one holds and those can become a little dogmatic. One may be feeling that what their partner believes is what they also believe, or they may think that their own beliefs have a significant impact on the relationship.

Hierophant represents partners who are happy, even if they subscribe to different religions. The relationship is able to work for both of them, with each one respecting what the other believes in, and not having a fear or need to control those beliefs. This relationship enables each partner to learn from the other and educates both in the different views held.

Also, the religious background of the partners has a significant influence on the relationship. The way the individuals were brought up and that surrounding environment has formulated their core belief system, starting from childhood and moving forward. Being conscious of how each person thinks and what actions are being implemented can be important things to consider when taking a step back to view how each partner interacts with the other. Sometimes, in communication, one may feel like they are "talking to a cement wall" when interacting with their partner. Both have their own ideas regarding how a relationship should be. This can go well or it can become an issue. If the relationship is in the beginning stages, one may be having doubts. Agreements can be made discussing how to respect each partner's boundaries without trying to change the other partner's belief system. This will offer a chance for the relationship to grow.

Marriage may be favorable for the desire of security and not being alone.

METAPHORICAL

Those of the Muslim faith do not eat pork because it's prohibited in the Quran. One may view that the pig eats anything for its food and the food processed isn't digested well enough, leaving the meat product unclean and unhealthy for consumption.

GENERAL MEANING FOR THE HIEROPHANT

- Open minded, rules that are written to be followed. (For example – Muslim married to or dating a Christian)
- Religion, partners who seek marriage counseling, stubborn in listening or taking action
- Education, women seeing a gynecologist for fertility conception, old belief system, stuck
- School, friends from different cultural or backgrounds, forgiveness

QUESTION STATEMENT:
What is one common belief you and your partner share?
How does this influence your relationship?

AFFIRMATION:
I love and accept my partner's differences.

TIMING:
1 week, 4th month, 5th month, April 20-May 20

The Lovers

ADAM AND EVE

Planet: Mercury – Talking and writing

Ruled by air sign Gemini: Mutable, *I am smart and clever*

7th Chakra: Crown – Meditation, all colors (white), or violet, or gold

Location: Central nervous system, top of head

The Lovers card represents the nature of sexuality that one has with another, with the excitement and passion that is felt in a relationship as both parties pursue the desire to connect on deeper intimate levels. One may have a more curious personality when it comes to desires. One may be inhibited and not likely to express their sexual desires out of fear or shame, including fear of what the partner would think or say about their desires, or shame of how cultural society views one's choices. For example, would partners be open to or reject the idea of playing dress up in the bedroom or trying different sexual positions? Would there be embarrassment for either partner?

Both partners made a decision to be together, whether the relationship is new or long term. They will find themselves putting the needed work into the relationship that it takes to move it forward. One may be easily tempted by the flirtation or seduction of other people; however, awareness of this, which makes this a workable situation, will help it pass. Actions of infidelity are unlikely to transpire at this time. The superficiality and losses that are involved within the partnership remind the partner that the consequences are not worth the loss of the relationship. Love is still there between you, as well. It can take the partner a little longer to admit, understand, or realize the true feelings towards the relationship.

Also, one minute the partner may want a commitment in the relationship; then, the next minute be unsure about what he or she really wants. Communication is stronger at this time regarding how each feels about the other and how partners feel as they express what feelings are felt, and what hidden insecurities are present at the moment. The general purpose of the relationship and meaning of what each partner wants within their unions can be found in conscious thought, having awareness in the choices made and how those choices impact the relationship and the partners. Are there physical connections, expressions of appreciation, like hugging your partner for 15 minutes a day, or communication via loving and respectful words to each other, the expression of gratitude for one another, thanks for taking the trash out, or for sweeping the floor? This can help with any frustration of being unappreciated.

METAPHORICAL

Ordering your favorite dessert, and enjoying every minute of it: There are many choices, but picking one and working within the selection allows you to pick the choice for your taste. Follow your bliss with passion.

GENERAL MEANING FOR THE LOVERS

- Choice, wants excitement in the relationship, trust your instinct about what going on
- Decisions, intelligent, resourceful, irresponsible actions
- Affinity, one who seeks superficial relationships for the thrill and excitement of them, good business
- Temptations, a person who meddles in the relationship and this results in conflict of interest, travel
- Financial success, someone making a decision in a committed relationship and never looking back

QUESTION STATEMENT:
Do your ideas of your sexuality harmonize with your actions of your relationship?

AFFIRMATION:
I make positive and healthy choices that support my growth
in life and surround my environment.

TIMING:
1 week, 6 months, Summer, May 21-June 20

The Chariot
A CRAB TRAVELING TO THE SEASHSHORE

Moon: Emotional reaction, intuition, monthly cycle, imagery gives an illusion

Ruled by Cancer: Cardinal, Betty Crocker – *I can be moody and clingy, but observant and caring*

1st Chakra: Sense of touch, color red

Location: Base, between genitals and anus

The Chariot can indicate a cancer-type personality. Also, one of the partners may be taking the relationship more seriously than the other. The Chariot depicts an archetype behavior: Who is the rescuer in the relationship? This shows a person who knows what they want out of life, the direction that needs to be taken, and is content with where the relationship is headed. There is very little emotion in decisions made for the relationship, thinking more with the mind instead of the heart.

In general, this is a good card for relationships. Each partner is able to learn from a past relationship or past problems and this has helped current communication. Drawing this card can indicate that each partner needs to have a little bit more of a sense of humor. Both people like to travel, and would like to travel more – more vacation time!

When talking about topics, it may be found that each has a strong view in what they believe in and each tries to domineer what the other one thinks. What one is thinking intuitively is likely the case in question. Partners may be wondering what the next move or step is for the relationship, or what actions will be taken after a decision is made. Someone may be indicated who is not accepting a decision that has been made in regards to the relationship, whether it is just to be friends, see other people, marriage, or space. Someone could be playing the rescuer in the relationship, trying to nurture or mother it and their partner, and, because of this, can create resentment.

METAPHORICAL

The Chariot card depicts a man or women on a chariot. The Shield of armor is equivalent to the shell of the crab – it protects one's inner self and allows one to move without emotion.

GENERAL MEANING FOR CHARIOT

- Travel, action, emotionless, narrow-minded, nurturing, domineering
- Plan, movement, humor, confidence, revenge, self centered, intuitive, vulnerable

QUESTION STATEMENT:
Are you on the same path as your partner in the relationship?
Or do you want the same things in the relationship as your partner?
What mistakes have you learned from in your relationship
that you can share with someone?
Who is using the words *Did you* or *I need you to*, to control the relationship?
Are you tailoring your conversation towards your partner's viewpoints?

AFFIRMATION:
I believe my relationship is moving into a healthier, happier environment.

TIMING:
The month of July, a week, a day, Sunday

Strength
CENTER OF ATTENTION

Sun: Reflects who you are

Ruled by Leo: Fixed fire sign – *I am vibrant, determined*

2nd Chakra: Expression, color Orange

Location: Reproductive area

Compassion and passion are felt or lacking in the relationship. One partner wants more heated energy, whereas the other is detached. Having patience with each other is the link to improving the dynamics between the two partners. One may be trying to play "the fixer" in the relationship and want to add their input about their partner and what they think needs improvement. Having creativity allows one to be expressive and keeps things fresh, steering away from boredom, which lessens the temptations of straying. One may unconsciously want their family and peer's approval for their relationship and who they picked as a partner. Part can be due to an insecurity and the other part may be how the relationship looks exteriorly. More value can be placed on superficiality than substance. When entering a relationship, one may tend to have unresolved issues from a past union, and when they enter the new situation, this causes them to create doubt and criticism about their current partner.

METAPHORICAL

Having a Persian cat as a pet: They require daily care and emotional interaction, brushing, cleaning the face, hugging. So does this relationship, embracing each other, express to your partner that you love them or appreciate them? Massaging your partners back or vice versa is an example. Your inner feelings are expressed outwardly through action. What are you reflecting back into the relationship?

GENERAL MEANING FOR STRENGTH

- Traveling locally, concerned about finances, high maintenance
- Having a sensitive conversation, one that is attracted to good looks, controls others
- Narcissism personality
- Associated with Leo astrological sign

QUESTION STATEMENT:
Are there any unresolved issues from the past that need work?

AFFIRMATION:
Real beauty comes from within.

TIMING:
July 23-August 22, 7th day, Sunday

The Hermit
A NIGHT TRAVELER

Ruled by Mercury: Reasoning
Planet: Virgo – Observant
3rd Chakra: Time out; color yellow
Location: Solar plexus, digestion

This relationship has taken more self-control and discipline in how one partner reacts emotionally to the other. One needs to look at how time away from the partner is spent. Indulge in some self-care – taking a bubble bath with lavender or another favorite scent, a massage, a haircut, manicure, or a walk. Reflect on what is appreciated in the relationship and what could be worked on. Send a written communication to your partner, possibly a text or email, or place a card in a pocket – expressing how much you love him or her.

This Tarot card reflects someone who has done a lot of self-reflection in the past and has worked on one's self regarding what a relationship means to them and knows what type of details are needed for the desired outcome. They have certain boundaries they search for to allow that connection with someone else.

There may be stress involved in the relationship; you may find that you or your partner may be staying home more or sleeping more. Depression may play a part in the relationship and may be idiopathic, with no known or a physiological cause, but this is temporary and will get better with help. You and your partner may be spending time alone with each other without external stimulation. Being alone with each other, souls can connect. There is a strong spiritual association with this card that depicts one being guided on a path that is naturally driven for personal growth.

Metaphorical

Preparing to take a backpacking trip into the mountain, one buys the sleeping bag, tent, utensils, shoes, flashlight and map. Setting out on the adventure of camping is fun, but it takes preparation.

GENERAL MEANING FOR HERMIT

- Isolated, business going well, metaphysical
- Quiet environment; no external stimulation or outside influences
- Stress, traveling by airplane, overnight stay, stressed out individuals
- Study, teaching, or professors, someone who likes to analyze details
- Medication, self-evaluation, worry, strain, anxiety, people with anxiety issues
- Searching within, Yoga, a need for relaxation
- Someone that is depressed mentally or by their surrounding environment

Question Statement:
What do you and your partner do with your time together?
What about time apart?
Remember it's the richness, the quality of the time spent together, not the quantity.

Affirmation:
I honor myself by meditating once a day.

Timing:
1 week, 9 months, August 23-September 22, mid-week, 3rd day, Wednesday

The Wheel of Fortune
BICYCLE WHEEL

Planet: Jupiter – Luck is with you

Ruled by Sagittarius: *I see*

4th Chakra: Conditional/unconditional love, color pink or green

Location: The center of the Heart

What makes up the nuts and bolts of the relationship? Is one *feeling* supportive or *being* supportive? How is the supportiveness being expressed to one another? For example, when one is overworked, does the partner help out with the household chores? When one is having a bad day, does the partner express empathic concern or a physical validation like a hug? Are the finances being respected, or are the decisions made being kept secret?

This card usually depicts a specific behavior or someone from the past who has resurfaced in the relationship. Fate and destiny are at work here; destiny is the action occurring in the relationship, like change of residence, new opportunities, and fate, which are the natural and unchangeable things that happen within each individual. For example, one can't change who gave birth to them or their ethnicity.

The relationship is in a healthier spiritual and supportive base than one has previous experienced. The cycle of fluctuation of feeling frustrated and stuck, then shifting to feelings of excitement and joy is a natural process that's taking shape in your relationship as a whole. It's like looking at a bicycle wheel and seeing what is in the center and how the spokes intertwine and hold the wheel together. The need to pay attention to the current focus in the relationship can be a good thing or bad thing for its progression. One may have a strong need to seek adventure and excitement, and the partner may strive to tear down that adventure, creating a tumultuous relationship.

Metaphorical

LOVE & PARTNER (FATE) = PLAN & ACTION (DESTINY)

A bicycle wheel is representative of a relationship, connected together by love that holds the axes and bearings (representing the partners), with the spokes being the plans that attach to the wheel to create a uniform wheel of action.

GENERAL MEANING FOR THE WHEEL OF FORTUNE

- Up-and-down cycles, new job in a new location, increased opportunities
- Fate, rewarding experience, promiscuous
- Destiny, having a balance in life, opportunities that need to be taken seriously
- Good luck, restless personality that becomes bored quickly
- Someone from the past, fearlessness, not wanting to settle down
- Magnitude, a decision or opportunity that leads to adventure

Question statement:
What holds the center of your relationship?

Affirmation:
I appreciate the cycle of my relationship and what can be learned from each lesson.

Timing:
1 week, 5th day, Thursday, November 22-December 21

Justice
WHEN TO BACK OFF

Planet: Venus – Possessions

Ruled by Libra air sign Libra: Cardinal – *I balance*, **fairness**

5th chakra: Forms of communication, color blue

Location: Throat

One may find that both partners, or just one, may easily bring forth feelings of fault in the relationship, affecting its efficiency. Communicating the way each partner feels and what could be worked out in a diplomatic way can ease the tightness in the relationship. The natural tendency to weigh all options when making decisions is a common theme. There is a need for more affection and the ability to learn that not winning all the arguments, or proving who is right or wrong in a conversation, is important. Lacking a definite position in what is wanted or expected may bring a sense of unease. This relationship is based on growth-affective communication, without the critic.

METAPHORICAL

Expressing how you really feel in a situation naturally allows the inner power to gain strength in authenticity.

GENERAL MEANING FOR JUSTICE

- Critical, complaining, articulate
- Watchful, uneasiness, right or wrong decisions
- Divorce, widow, decisions made out of gender

QUESTION STATEMENT:
Are you accepting your partner as they are or do you have an ideal in what you think they *should* be?

AFFIRMATION:
I love listening to my partner's point of view without judgment, which enables my relationship to propel forward in a healthy and supportive environment.

TIMING:
1 week, 5th day, Friday, Fall, August 23-September 22

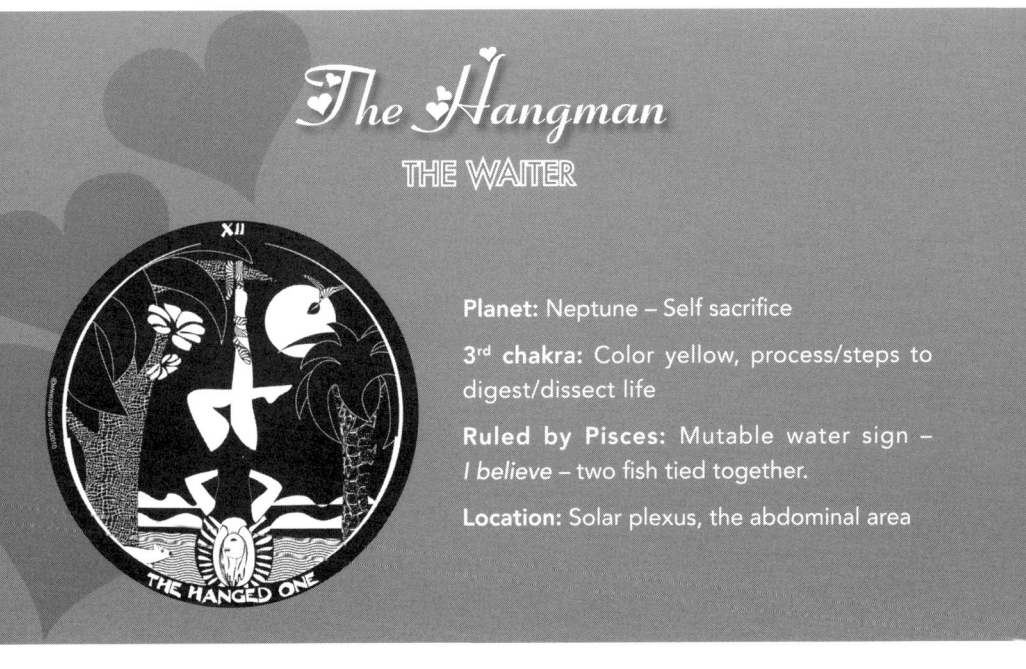

The Hangman
THE WAITER

Planet: Neptune – Self sacrifice

3rd chakra: Color yellow, process/steps to digest/dissect life

Ruled by Pisces: Mutable water sign – *I believe* – two fish tied together.

Location: Solar plexus, the abdominal area

There is a sense of loss of direction regarding where the relationship is currently headed. There is a need to see things more clearly. The movement of the relationship, or the feeling between the two partners, is stagnating. Decisions need to be made that may cause the relationship to come to a halt. You or your partner have made sacrifices to adjust. There may be a lack of structure, giving it the feeling of being stuck in the dark. Talking to your partner or another source for advice regarding what you're feeling stuck about can give you new ideas for your situation. Also, be willing to listen, even if that means that you may have to be open to what your partner is feeling or wanting. Working on the *why you feel stuck* and what you or your partner have sacrificed in an open-ended communication, not expecting to win the conversation, will help bring the relationship to a new place. There are two different thoughts in this relationship, very different directions; each partner has their own idea regarding how the relationship should be.

Metaphorical

Make the necessary sacrifices for a goal that is desired by choice. Taking a class to learn a new subject will require one to study and prioritize a schedule for success. This sacrifice is a choice, just like being in a relationship with a particular partner who brings a rearrangement of what life used to be.

GENERAL MEANING FOR THE HANGMAN

- Suspension, waiting on a decision from someone else before you can take action
- New opportunities, sacrifices made to be in a particular relationship, need to make a decision
- Changes occurring in life, making money that entails a waiting or grace period, conflicting actions

QUESTION STATEMENT:
What is one thing that you feel is making you feel stuck in your relationship?

AFFIRMATION:
I don't live my life through other people's views; I enjoy thinking outside the box.

TIMING:
1 week, Thursday, February 21-March 20

Death
NEW HAIR COLOR

Planet: Pluto – transformation

Ruled by water sign Scorpio: Fixed, *I desire*

7th Chakra: Listen to your ESP, all colors (white), or violet, gold

Location: Located above your head in the crown area

This card represents change that needs to happen, or has already taken place, in the relationship. For things that need to change, it's either some old, bad patterns that are inhibiting the growth of the relationship or bad habits that are causing inhibition to one's personal growth. Making a conscious action to change the patterns needs to be put into focus along with a strategy that has careful planning. One may feel that part of the relationship is controlled by an outside factor, like a partner's work schedule. Resentment and suspicion develop when one partner puts more focus on their personal career, which creates separation and less emphasis on the relationship. Unresolved issues may be a theme with an ex-partner that sparks a feeling of nostalgia. Going separate ways for a time to learn about one's co-dependency can enable one to see clearer in the relationship. For example, I like being in a relationship for the personal company of what that person gives me: comfort and companionship. I don't like being alone, even if the relationship causes me to change.

METAPHORICAL

Changing hair color can achieve a subtle new look, which brings a positive feeling of self esteem. In relationships, changing bad behaviors can set the relationship to a new level of happiness.

GENERAL MEANING FOR DEATH

- Change, manipulation, willpower
- Divorce, determination, successful business women
- Widow, transformation, men who can be violent
- Suspicion, separation, traveling to different countries for work

Question Statement:
How does your partner feel about your success?
What is an old behavior that can be addressed in the relationship?

Affirmation:
I will succeed; I have the willpower and determination.

Timing:
1 week, 9 week or months, Wednesday, 10 weeks or months, fall

Temperance
WATERFALL

Planet: Jupiter – Abundance

Ruled by fire sign Sagittarius: Mutable – wanderer, *I seek adventure.*

4th Chakra: Desires, color green or pink

Location: Chest area

This is a card of patience and moderation. There may be a need to balance your emotional display in actions you take towards the relationship. You may have found that there has been a period of waiting things out, holding back your emotions, masking emotions, and seeing if this relationship is a fit. The need to balance emotions like fear, anger, and love are needed. The pouring of the water represents the consciousness of the emotions and the ability to be aware of the emotional actions you and your partner bring forth, as well as understanding the way they are sent and received by one another. You may find that your partner is holding back in the relationship, due to the desire for independence and the fear of losing an independent and adventurous life. Also, an involvement of mixed diversities like cultural or ethnic influence is indicated. Learning to balance and intertwine the differences with the awareness of adaptability creates a successful growth. Knowing what you're flexible in, listening without interference, having confidence in one's own ability, and having insight into the problem in order to adapt are keys to an effective adaptability.

METAPHORICAL

Receiving gifts can be fun and appreciated. Getting a gift that one is not that happy with, but still smiling and saying thank you for the thoughtfulness allows the receiver to maintain a balanced response without hurting the giver.

GENERAL MEANING FOR TEMPERANCE

- Patience, adventures
- Balance, mixed emotions
- Emotions, mixed ethnicity

QUESTION STATEMENT:
How are your emotions expressed in the relationship?

AFFIRMATION:
I'm aware of all of my emotions.

TIMING:
1 week, Thursday, 11 months, 12 months, winter

The Devil
FAMOUS TENNIS PLAYER

Planet: Saturn – Facing fears and ambition, structure

Ruled by earth sign Capricorn: Cardinal, *I use*

5th Chakra: Communicate free and openly, color blue

Location: Throat

The Devil card usually depicts a women and a man in chains held together. You or your partner may be having vices or hang ups, meaning an activity or an action that can cause hindrance in the relationship. For example, someone could be spending too much money, be involved with a drug or sex addiction, have anger issues, or be argumentative. These vices will appear in the relationship and bring awareness of the behavior that needs adjusting.

Also, a special connection between you and your partner is felt. There may be a codependency in the relationship, whether it's financial or emotional. Having a clear understanding about what your partner and you want in the relationship is needed. Having the ability to listen to your partner (and vice versa) and being able to listen and work on the needed changes will help.

Metaphorical

It may be that a person has a squeaky-clean image around their peers, but is found later to have been a part of a scandal and not the image portrayed in public. The addictions that people have can lead them to act out in a destructive manner for themselves and for their partner(s).

GENERAL MEANING FOR THE DEVIL

- Special attraction, abuse of power or position
- Codependency, cheating behind a spouse's back
- Addictions, numbing feelings and emotions
- Jealousy, ethnical culture

Question statement:
What is one thing that you depend upon in the relationship from your partner?

Affirmation:
I love myself – enough to not self-abandon my personal needs.

Timing:
1 week, 13 days, Saturday, December 22-January 19

BUILDING A HOUSE

Planet: Mars – Psychical energy

Ruled by fire sign Aries: Cardinal – straight forward. *I am.*

1st Chakra: Safety and security of home life, color red

Location: Base of the spine

The relationship security and safety is in question here. There may be new feelings that make your partner feel uncomfortable. You may have met your partner unexpectedly and this took you completely by surprise. Also, you and your partner may be stepping *out of the box* when it comes to a completely different kind of relationship. It's important to look at the relationship and what was founded in the beginning; for example: Was your relationship founded on both parties wanting a committed relationship? Dishonesty causes loss of security when it is not founded on stability or wanting a committed relationship. Being in a relationship makes one feel safe, even if it involves not paying attention to what is really right for you and accepting a relationship that doesn't allow for you to grow or pay attention to your own personal needs. So when unexpected events take place, it takes you by complete surprise.

As the relationship progresses, you will learn new things from and about your partner that you never knew before, like what they like and dislike, or whether he or she really wanted to be in a faithful, committed relationship, but was only in the relationship with you temporarily for their own emotional security and safety issues. The questions of a partner's old ways changing may involve his or her outgrowing old habits because of a change in social development or residence. Also, your partner may be full of anger, which disrupts the relationship.

METAPHORICAL

When one is standing on a rug and a friend comes along and pulls the rug from beneath them, their stability and sense of security is lost – taking them completely by surprise.

GENERAL MEANINGS FOR THE TOWER

- Lies, anger, enlightened from an unexpected event
- Unexpected change, end of a relationship
- Change in employment, finances, residence, or relationships
- New habits, unexpected events

QUESTION STATEMENT:
What has taken you by complete surprise in the relationship, and is it workable between you and your partner?
In the beginning of the relationship, were past relationships and ideas discussed, and are they in the past?
Does your partner really want a committed relationship?

AFFIRMATION:
I want an open and honest relationship.

TIMING:
1 week, 2 days, Tuesday, March 20-April 18

The Star
TROPICAL ISLAND

Planet: Uranus – Independence

Ruled by air sign Aquarius: Fixed, *I know*

2nd Chakra: Element of water; love, fear, and hate, color orange

Location: Reproductive area

In the relationship, open communication is easy and this brings a sense of encouragement as the relationship progresses. There is a sense of understanding each other's emotions, whether it's love for certain things, like food, taste in movies or activities, or hating the same things – this gives both partners a feeling of openness. Having the ability to understand where your partner's emotions are coming from gives you a feeling of encouragement that the relationship will work out in the long run.

METAPHORICAL

The feeling when being asked out by your current partner brought excitement and anticipation. The zest you felt with the first kiss between you, was bliss! There's a "vibe" with your partner.

GENERAL MEANING FOR THE STAR

- Hope, good luck, having self-doubt in one's ability
- Encouragement, artist, being inspired by new opportunities
- Connection, fair complexion, emotional satisfaction
- New beginning, understating of one's emotions

QUESTION STATEMENT:
When was the last time you and your partner were thinking of the same thing, like wanting to do the same activity?

AFFIRMATION:
I thank my lucky stars.

TIMING:
1 week, winter, 1 or 2 months, first of the year, Sunday

The Moon
FULL MOON

Planet: Neptune – Wholeness

Moon: Full, waxing, waning

Ruled by water sign Pisces: Mutable – compassionate, *I dream*

6th Chakra: Perception through intuition, color indigo

Location: 3rd eye, mid-brain

A person with an astrology water sign is indicated, like Pisces. There are a lot of intuitional feelings that are felt in the relationship, and your partner may have changeable moods – one day happy, another day down; or one day wants a committed relationship, another day unsure of the commitment. Also, what you may be thinking is going on in your relationship between you and your partner may not be the case. Neglecting to acknowledge the real facts in the relationship is ignored because of someone's self-esteem. This card is about being and staying in a relationship with a partner who is not ready for commitment, and who is there due to their own insecurity and low self-esteem issues. Accepting what's really going on between you and your partner will allow you to accept the facts and make necessary choices. The partner you are with can be very sensitive, or this is a very sensitive time for you and your partner. Things are not what they seem; something is going on behind your back. The ability to be very creative in the relationship gives one partnership a sense of security. Opportunistic ideals may be the reason why your partner stays in the relationship.

METAPHORICAL

When your closet door is open and the light is dim, your jacket looks like someone standing there; but when the light is on, the illusion is exposed and you see that it is just your jacket. The moon's reflection brings enlightenment into one's consciousness.

GENERAL MEANING FOR THE MOON

- Lies, imagination
- Deceit, emotions are interfering with work
- Intuition, movie lovers
- Not accepting the reality, influence is based on not true friends

QUESTION STATEMENT:
What is one thing that you may be ignoring in the relationship, and that you intuitively are feeling?

AFFIRMATION:
I give thanks to the moon for all its intuitive energy.

TIMING:
1 week, Thursday, 2 months to 3 months, February 21-March 20

The Sun
CANDLE THAT IS LIT

Sun: Essential self

Ruled by fire sign Leo: Fixed – center of attention, *I show.*

3rd Chakra: Self-esteem/responsibility, ego, power, authority, color yellow

Location: Solar plexus, stomach area

Hope and courage are two themes of this relationship. No matter what state or where the relationship is currently, you and your partner are hopeful that things will work out for both of you. Whether you're engaged or getting a divorce, both of you are at the point where you're getting what is needed, meaning both your self-esteem and needs are being met, along with the responsibility you're taking with one another. Even though the future of the relationship may not be clear – for instance, setting an exact date on marriage, selling a house, or finalizing an important event in your life – you're aware of what steps you need to take as an individual to get closer to the goal of your relationship.

Relatives around you, or your partner's family, may focus on too much of the external appearance or accomplishments of you or your partner; this may be culturally how it has been for many years. One needs to ask who has the authority in the relationship.

This can indicate that your partner may not be being feeling appreciated at times; saying thank you to your partner can make them feel valued.

METAPHORICAL

As long as the candle has a flame, there is light that gives insight to any problem. Light has a natural ability to add warmth to any darkness.

GENERAL MEANING FOR THE SUN

- Happy in the outcome, delays in marriage, having doubts
- Satisfaction with each other, success in exams due to staying focused
- Opportunities at work/career, retaking exams due to being distracted
- Engaged women, positive thinking helps with depression
- A divorce that has a new Happiness for life

Question statement:
What is one thing that is clear in your situation, and what is one thing that is not clear?

Affirmation:
I love and appreciate the Sun's warmth and how it brings joy into my life.

Timing:
1 week, Sunday, 7th day or 8th month, late summer, July 23-August 22

Judgment
VISITING IN-LAWS

Plant: Pluto – transformer into light that reveals

Ruled by water sign Scorpio: Fixed – *I dig deep into the depths of the universe.* Holding on to a secret that will be revealed later

7th Chakra: Peak level of consciousness, all colors (white), violet, gold

Location: Crown area above your head

Changes are occurring in the relationship, and with this, bringing fear of an unknown outcome. The changes taking place are from actions and events that have happened in the past. Now, an unexpected situation has occurred, forcing the issues from the past to be addressed, which will ultimately bring change to the relationship. In the past, your partner may have procrastinated, taking actions because they were afraid of what could happen. One may have difficulty expressing affection; this can be from unconscious repression. One may have grown up in an environment that had repression of affection, which leads to suppression of feelings. Working on this will give mental clarity. If being judged, one needs to ask themselves to identify the stimulant for the judgment: Is it the internal discomfort with that particular situation that's being judged, or is it unresolved issues in one's life that are propelling the judgment? Internal discomfort with certain actions or situations can cause one to judge. These can be unresolved issues in one's life becoming the catalyst for the judgment. Letting go of old beliefs or understanding why they are internal stimulants can bring awareness. The ability to let go of old beliefs or customs that allow an improvement in your relationship. You or your partner may be keeping hidden information about your relationship and not revealing anything too personal; however, a situation will occur that will cause what has been buried from a third party to come to light, due to an inevitable change of circumstances which will improve the relationship. Your partner may be too caught up with how someone in particular will judge the relationship. Being a good listener will allow your partner to feel more comfortable with a secret without being judged, having understanding about reactions to certain events affecting emotions. Someone around the relationship may have a "belief" in how things are done (like a map); this can cause hidden issues.

Metaphorical

The battery is a device that changes the current energy in the light bulb that represents the relationship between you and your partner. It is the circumstances that initiate the situation.

GENERAL MEANING FOR JUDGMENT

- New job, situation/circumstances that need to be addressed/acknowledged
- Advancement in employment, confusion about one's self or what decision to take
- Improved condition, hindrance due to one's own actions
- Illness that has been ignored, being judged because you're following your own desire
- Procrastination due to fear, favorable outcomes
- Invisible, hidden

Question statement:
Do you respect your partner's perspective and are you non-judgmental in how actions affect others?

Affirmation:
I'm open to my emotions and feeling.

Timing:
1 week, Thursday, 10 months, 11 months, fall, October 24-November 21

The World
GLOBE

Planet: Saturn – organization and discipline

Ruled by earth sign Capricorn: Cardinal – *I put together.* Lacks humor, mature, the CEO

1st, 2nd, 3rd, 4th, 5th, 6th, 7th **Chakras:** Run midline through the body, from the top of the crown to the base of the urogenital area, color violet

This is a card of completion, an end of a cycle that leads to a new start from a new perspective and fresh beginning. Lessons were learned in the past in your relationship that allowed for you and your partner to feel complete. You may have dealt with a partner who didn't see the same problems in the relationships as you did, but with time, he or she wanted to get away from the dysfunctional feelings and move towards stability. With the ability to listen to your partner's points (and vice versa), and the ability to give constructive feedback when needed, the relationship was able to move forward out of the slumps. There still may be work to be done with the communication and planning. Starting work in the relationship is a continuous process and your partner may have forgotten that the work between you and him or her is ongoing. The relationship needs to change with the changing circumstances.

METAPHORICAL

When running in a marathon, it takes discipline to get into shape and to train the mind and body for endurance. Having a structured schedule allows one to succeed (to completion) with what they set out to do.

GENERAL MEANING FOR THE WORLD

- Completion, achievement, coming from a family of divorce
- End of a cycle, movement, need to laugh more
- Stagnation, travel, doesn't express emotions, hides feelings viewing them as weak

QUESTION STATEMENT:
Do you feel like your relationship has gone from start to finish?

AFFIRMATION:
I thank the Universe for all the life lessons that I can learn from.

TIMING:
1 week, Saturday, December 22-January 19

Chapter 3
The Seasonal Arcane

Ace of Cups
NEW BEGINNINGS

Season: Northern Hemisphere summertime

1st Chakra: The emotional connection you had as a child with your parents has a role in this chakra and card, color red

Location: Base of the spine area

New beginnings are the foundation of Ace of Cups. The relationship can be in either of two phases. In one, the honeymoon phase is full of fun, excitement, thrills and enjoyment of each other in the relationship, which creates superficial emotional support at that period. The second phase of the relationship is adaptability. When the relationship goes more in depth, the couple learns more about each other – their dislikes, their likes. As these layers unfold, they can create a need to adapt to the changes that are going on in the relationship and within themselves. As each partner evolves, views and perception on things can change. Or, has the relationship lost its fizz and spark, with feelings of desires unfulfilled? The intention at the beginning of the relationship has to be asked: Did the partnership start out as just sexual attraction, or was there more of an intellectual appeal? Was someone a rescuer, wanting to save or fix a partner, or be involved with codependency for security? If the relationship is unfulfilled, first, the person(s) has to take inventory within themselves to see if they're happy with themselves. Are they secure with what they are doing in life? Sometimes, the problem isn't with the partner; it's with the person looking at the situation – they project the unhappiness onto their partner, playing the blame game and creating resentment. Having open communication, asking how the other partner feels, and seeing if something can be changed between the two partners is important. Getting involved with hobbies together, spending time with one another, like taking walks, can help. It's a sensitive issue, and listening with respect is a start to see where the relationship can go.

METAPHORICAL

The fizz in soda is what makes the beverage peppy, but when it loses this peppiness, the drink becomes flat. In the beginning of a relationship or venture, the feeling of excitement is there, but with time it can beginning to dwindle.

GENERAL MEANING FOR ACE OF CUPS

- Getting a project deal, traveling brings good luck, someone focused on quantity versus quality
- Your proposal gets a yes, work/career is going good, being late to an appointment
- Getting pregnant, finances start out great, then taper off
- Arguments about not being on time/time efficient
- Going to a counselor, a situation that needs more clarity before making a decision

QUESTION STATEMENT:
What makes your relationship fulfilling? Unfulfilled?

AFFIRMATION:
As I breathe in and out, I fulfill myself with love and care.

TIMING:
June, July, August

INTENTION REACTIONS

Season: Northern Hemisphere wintertime

1st Chakra: Root of intention and reaction, open communication expressed between you and your parents growing up is key, color red

Location: Base of the spine area

The intention behind your words and the way you communicate with your partner – verbally, or nonverbally – and the reaction or actions that are carried out is the theme of this card. When partners communicate with each other, there is a point of origin that forms messages that are carried out. Whether they're happy, sad, angry, or resentful, these are the catalysts of the interactions between the couple. When a person has an awareness of knowing why they have the feelings they have, and are conscious in how they act with their partner, this creates healthy communication and self-esteem in the relationship. Issues can stem from early childhood or past traumas that resurface. For example, past traumas cause the person to have intimacy issues with their partner because they already feel violated, and when the person shuts down, physically, the other partner feels rejected – one partner feels like a victim and the other rejected. A lighter example is a partner just having a bad day, or a great day, angry or happy, because their boss or clients made them feel frustrated or satisfied. Then, when they see their partner, they recreate how they felt at work and treat their partner in the same manner. Intentions comes from what one desires, whether it is being nice or vengeful. Before you speak, take five seconds and ask yourself: Okay, what am I trying to create out of this communication? Is it to make my partner feel what I'm feeling?

METAPHORICAL

When your partner is under the weather, you bring then some warm soup, your intention being to make them feel better. They respond in gratitude and appreciation.

GENERAL MEANING FOR ACE OF SWORDS

- This is an important time when decisions are made, travel that brings unexpected change of thought
- Career moves, opportunities go well, depth of love, difficulty getting pregnant
- Working in a male-dominate environment, competition, arguments, male ego
- New cycle of the way one thinks and speaks, a job that gives one control, money, but does make one happy

QUESTION STATEMENT:
Are you aware how your words have an effect on your health and life.

AFFIRMATION:
When I speak, I use words of support, compassion, and understanding.

TIMING:
December, January, February

Ace of Pentacles
PROSPERITY THROUGH MANIFESTATION

Season: Northern Hemisphere fall-time

1st Chakra: The stability of one's household when growing up as a child, moving or staying in the same environment, color red

Location: Base of the spine area

Strong ambition and career goals are the themes and origins of Ace of Pentacles. In the relationship, both partners are career driven and love what money brings – all the materialism that one can buy. Physicality is more important to one partner than the other. Sexuality comfortably comes up in this card. One partner may enjoy exploring and expressing different methods or ways to connect, whereas the other partner hasn't been exposed to that kind of thinking, and may not be comfortable with it, or doesn't like a particular situation. One example might be kissing your partner after oral sex – your partner may be shocked.

The idea of financial security is focused in this relationship, where other important needs are ignored, like partners who are solely attentive on their careers and yet they have minimal or nonexistent physical intimacy. For example, no touching or hugging in the relationship becomes their norm.

METAPHORICAL

When we plant seeds in a garden or buy a new plant, basic nourishment is required for it to grow, such as water (emotions), soil (growth) and food (communication).

GENERAL MEANING FOR ACE OF PENTACLES

- Goals that are reached, feeling fulfilled in the work one does
- Internet dating, dating two people at the same time, one that likes to plan ahead
- Excellent finances, dull person focused on wealth/accomplishment

QUESTION STATEMENT:
What is the focus of your relationship?

AFFIRMATION:
I embrace a balanced life.

TIMING:
March, April, May

Ace of Wands
AMBITION BRINGS NEW PLANS

Season: Northern Hemisphere springtime

1st Chakra: The creativity of the home growing up, color red

Location: Base of the spine area

Creativity, passion, leadership, and ambition is the source of Ace of Wands. Partners give full attention to the relationship by showing their concern and by communicating their caring words and support for each other. This is a starting time and it can be a new relationship, or feel like it's a new relationship, even though the partners may have been together for a while. It is a time when the couple sets their ideas and plans for the future.

Also, one can be driven by the excitement and attraction, and love being *in* a relationship, but when one partner doesn't meet expectations, then the other may take it hard, and begin to wallow in self-doubt. For example, one can have a partner who makes a great husband or wife – they're attentive, loving, and respectful – but they may not be as talkative or spontaneous. This is what the opposite partner considers lacking, and what really *gets* to them. The partner is failing to see all the great qualities in their mate and focusing only on one or two characteristics. When one puts too much emphasis on a particular thing, this "hang up" is a hidden issue showing what they are really feeling within themselves, and they project that onto their partner. Also, some may be in a relationship just to *be* in a relationship, or they don't want to be alone, so he or she "settles" for what is around.

Metaphorical

When starting a business, management teams use the acronym SMART to help begin accomplishing goals. This can help in relationships, too. For example, *S* for being specific in what you want, *M* for measuring the time, *A* to see if your plans are attainable, *R* for recording your progress, and *T* for time management.

Be specific with your plan, measure your plan, see if your plan is attainable, record your progress and time. Be SMART.

GENERAL MEANING FOR ACE OF WANDS

- Making plans, but not following through, a great time to travel
- Having doubts in one's ability, career and finances are going well
- Written rules, the source of an idea that leads to learning

Question statement:
What are some things that are going great in your relationship?

Affirmations:
I'm the source of my happiness.

Timing:
September, October, November

Chapter 4
The Pip Cards

2 of Cups
ASSOCIATED WITH ADAPTABLE VS INCOMPATIBLE

2nd Chakra: Orange color, element of water
Meaning: Incompatibility/Compatibility
Location: Reproductive area

    This card focuses on coming together in a relationship, but seeing things on a different level regarding the way that relationship should be. One partner wants things one way, and the other, another. For example, one partner likes a lot of attention and phone calls and texts throughout the day, and the other one likes only one phone call a day. Not *seeing eye to eye*, or wanting varied things, can create incompatibility due to differences and the inability to compromise and talk about the expression of feelings. One may be self-absorbed, not interested in listening to other views; there can be sexual incompatibility; you may like a new type of intimacy, while your partner is not comfortable trying new things. In Communication, one partner can be more hurtful in the way they express themselves, or their views.

    Look at your relationship with humor; balance the responsibility (i.e., who is paying for what, who does the cleaning, etc.). In compatibility, mutual interest is experienced and shared in this relationship – partners may share the same life views, like the same movies, food, politics, religion, or they may have a strong desire to be together despite some differences.

Metaphorical

Coca Cola has many flavors for their beverage: Some people like Diet Coke, regular Coke, or Coke Zero. They like Coca Cola and want the beverage, but they want a different kind of flavor.

General Meaning for 2 of Cups

- Being in a relationship with a different cultural person, wanting marriage
- Attraction to each other physically, easily sensitive to emotional events/words
- Travel to a near location, withholds emotions
- Success in money matters, easily walked over or take advantage
- Misjudgment, unionships
- Shared desires, arguments due to personality differences

Question statement:
What is one desire, or desires, you share with your partner?

Affirmation:
I express my desires with love and acceptance.

Timing:
2 days, 2 weeks, 2 months, 2nd day of the week

2 of Swords
ASSOCIATED WITH RESTRICTION VS ASSERTION

2nd Chakra: Orange color, element of resistence

Meaning: Intelligence and reason

Location: Reproductive area

The relationship dynamics show inconsistencies of wants and needs among each partner, which brings an unknown direction and mixed emotions of anguish or frustration. One minute your partner is full of expression regarding how they feel, and then the next, they withdraw.

You know what action to take or what can be done to improve the relationship, but then there comes a standstill or halt. One, though, has learned from past relationships and understands the importance of working together, and understands what can come from learning about each other. Movement is indicated; more needs to be known before decisions can be made. There is a decision that needs to be made in regards to the relationship; the difficulty of making the decision is based on logic or emotions. The anguish lies within, in thought patterns, and creating a new plan will help you to move out of the burdensome circumstances.

METAPHORICAL

When the grocery market runs a special on their produce, does one break a weekly schedule and stop by the market to shop, or do they stick with their current routine? Sometimes, decisions are not easily made.

GENERAL MEANING FOR 2 OF SWORDS:

- In a rut, reasoning out a problem, refusing to see the reality of the circumstances
- Good news with a job or finances, feeling of not being sure, new and unexpected opportunities
- Intelligence, petty arguments or disagreements, instability of emotions, confusion

QUESTION STATEMENT:
When communicating with your partner,
which is easier: through affection, words, or gifts?

AFFIRMATION:
When I feel resistance in my life I surrender to the Higher Source/God.

TIMING:
2 days, 2 weeks, 2 months, 2nd day of the week, September 23-October 22

2 of Wands
ASSOCIATED WITH CONCLUSIVE VS INDECISIVE

2nd Chakra: Orange color, element of love
Meaning: See-saw, pulley system
Location: Reproductive area

This is a time for a decision, or decisions, to be made regarding what actions need to be taken. Partners may be indecisive in what direction to go. The indecisions come from questioning whether their skills or creativity will be used well, or if this is the right path for them. One partner may not be sure where the relationship is headed – is this full commitment going to last, and if it *is* a commitment, what is the next step? The other may not have decided whether they really want the relationship and could be waiting to see what other opportunities are available. The back-and-forth thinking can be because of the immaturity of the person, i.e., not being ready to take the responsibility of a relationship, or by being open to another person and allowing themselves to be vulnerable. Additionally, they may not be able to accept another person's faults, or be open and willing to listen to new ideas and opinions from another. One may be involved with a personality that can be fun and joking at times, but can allow their anger or frustration to build up over time, becoming explosive in an argument. When things do not work out for them as they planned, they can project their discomfort and tantrums onto their partner and make the home environment tense. One wants to make a decision, but is concerned about what the partner will do and how they would react. Better to work through the indecisions and make decisions which allow both partners to go through a problem in the moment and allow the relationship to benefit from the action in the future.

Metaphorical

Playing on the see-saw as a child brought joy and adventure. Going up and down with the see-saw has a hint of fear and excitement which can be felt in a relationship.

GENERAL MEANING FOR THE 2 OF WANDS

- Dominant personality that causes restriction or hindrance, travel over water, new country, stranded
- Arrogance which leads to disagreements, a problem works out for the better
- A new opportunity for a new job, stop procrastinating
- Applying to a new career or school program, business deals going good

Question statement:
What is one thing that keeps going back and forth in your relationship?

Affirmation:
I'm thankful for sharing and making healthy decisions together with my partner, showing respect and admiration for each other.

Timing:
2 days, 2 weeks, 2 months, 2nd day of the week

2 of Pentacles
ASSOCIATED WITH ONWARD VS DOWNWARD

2nd Chakra: Orange color, element of fear
Meaning: Slow, short, baby steps
Location: Reproductive area

In the beginning of the relationship, one may tend to take things slowly. They are happy to act with reserve in their actions, like expressing how they feel or making a full commitment with their partner. This might be the first time that one has entered a relationship that has the full potential for a long-lasting commitment or marriage. One may be too focused on "is this the one?" creating back-and-forth commitment between the two. Both partners are attracted towards each other and share similar values. One may be more reserved with their displayed emotions and not quick to express their feelings, and, at times, can be stubborn. Both partners share a similar work ethic and can be competitive. Having patience with your partner and supporting their "speed" in the way they progress into the relationship will help develop the bond between the two.

METAPHORICAL:

Walking a tight rope takes time. The rope is securing your relationship, but it takes time to walk to the other side on the rope. The rope represents the commitment of the relationship and requires adaptability.

GENERAL MEANING FOR 2 OF PENTACLES

- Adaptability, shy, money comes and goes, more than one occupation
- Overburdened, traveling may be slow, flexibility, juggling jobs or money
- Not expressing emotional feelings in public, interference/misrepresented from a past coworker

QUESTION STATEMENT:
What new changes were made to be together and how do you and your partner feel about it?

AFFIRMATION:
With every step I take, it's a positive step in the right direction.

TIMING:
2 days, 2 weeks, 2 months, 2nd day of the week, December 21-January 20

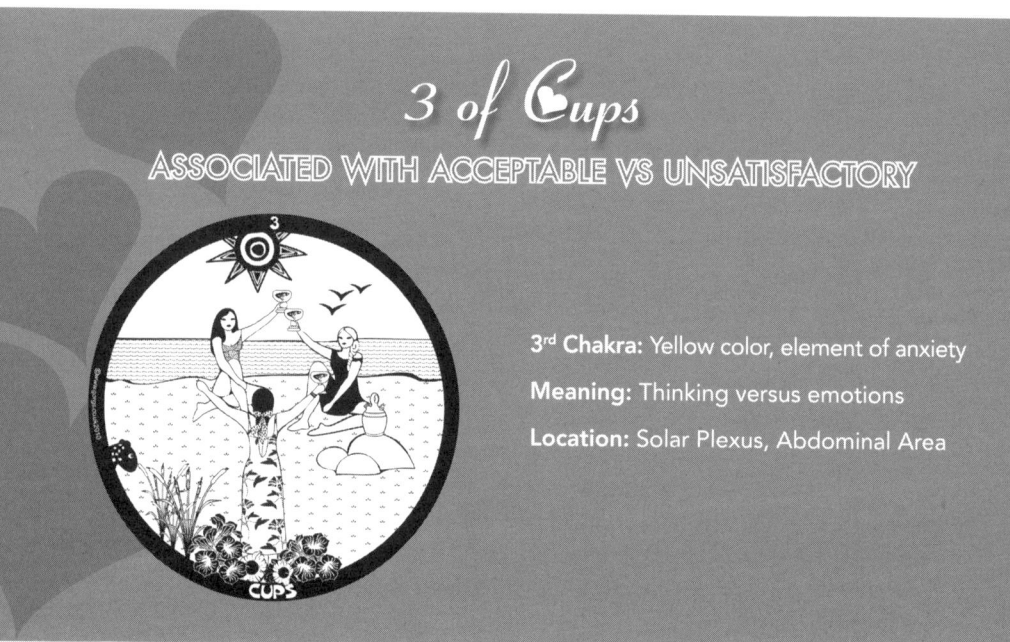

3 of Cups
ASSOCIATED WITH ACCEPTABLE VS UNSATISFACTORY

3rd Chakra: Yellow color, element of anxiety
Meaning: Thinking versus emotions
Location: Solar Plexus, Abdominal Area

The relationship can be full of satisfaction at one moment; then the next, there is a level of uncertainty, as the relationship has turned to another tide. One partner may not be appreciated and could feel unsatisfied, forcing them to lash out and make immature decisions. The partner is seeking emotional fulfillment lacking in the relationship – even if it's through *one-night stands* or superficial get-togethers. The uncertainty of direction was co-created, whether it was by being faithful or cheating. Emotional connecting with your partner, allowing thoughts, desires, and fears brings more fulfillment. This card depicts times when things can go really great...or seriously wrong. A person can be going through a rebound and looking for superficial relationships to fill a current void where there is numbness due to the change and transition of their status now being single.

GENERAL MEANING FOR 3 OF CUPS

- Getting a supervisory job, celebration
- Not getting a teaching job (they are not seeing your talent), cheating
- Anniversary, picking a partner who is promiscuous
- Having good luck in a financial transaction, hearing good news

METAPHORICAL:

Going on a sunny Caribbean island for vacation can be fun and relaxing; then, in the middle of it, the air conditioner breaks down, so frustration and confusion can be felt. Should one leave their quarters to go to another unit?

QUESTION STATEMENT:
Do you have a "check-in time" with your partner to find out what's going on with them – how are they feeling about news, events, their career, or health?

AFFIRMATION:
I celebrate life lessons.

TIMING:
3 days, 3 weeks, 3 months, 3rd day of the week, June 21-July 21

3 of Swords
ASSOCIATED WITH APPREHENSION VS ASSURED

3rd Chakra: Yellow Color, element of assimilating

Meaning: Protecting one's feelings

Location: Solar plexus, abdominal area

    This card represents the isolating of one's self by not entering into a relationship due to a past hurt, or being in a relationship and not fully sharing your life with that partner because of the fear of how it will affect one's life. Work still needs to be done if both parties are willing to listen to each other; if not, then parting ways may be a choice. The issue or issues going on have been causing disappointment for a while. One needs to look at themselves and not at their partner; the only thing that can be controlled is one's own behavior – not a partner's. The actions of the partner may have not been fair to the relationship, or to their partner, or there may be dependency issues. In a codependent relationship, you will see one partner doing all the work, seeking the attention, and trying to make or fix the issues, and the other partner not involved with the relationship at all. There are many issues that bring about codependency situations: self-abandonment issues, financial strain, low self-esteem, or growing up with a codependent parent.

METAPHORICAL

    Swimming is a healthy and enjoyable experience; however, it can be scary and fearful for some people trying to learn to swim. Past experiences could come into play to exacerbate the fear.

GENERAL MEANING FOR 3 OF SWORDS

- Disappointment, surgery, narcissistic neurotic behavior
- Divorce, feeling alienated, grief due to an end of something
- Cheating, working on a project for a long time, refusing to see the reality of the situation

QUESTION STATEMENT:
What has caused disappointment in the relationship?

AFFIRMATION:
I look within for my happiness.

TIMING:
3 days, 3 weeks, 3 months, 3rd day of the week, September 23-October 22

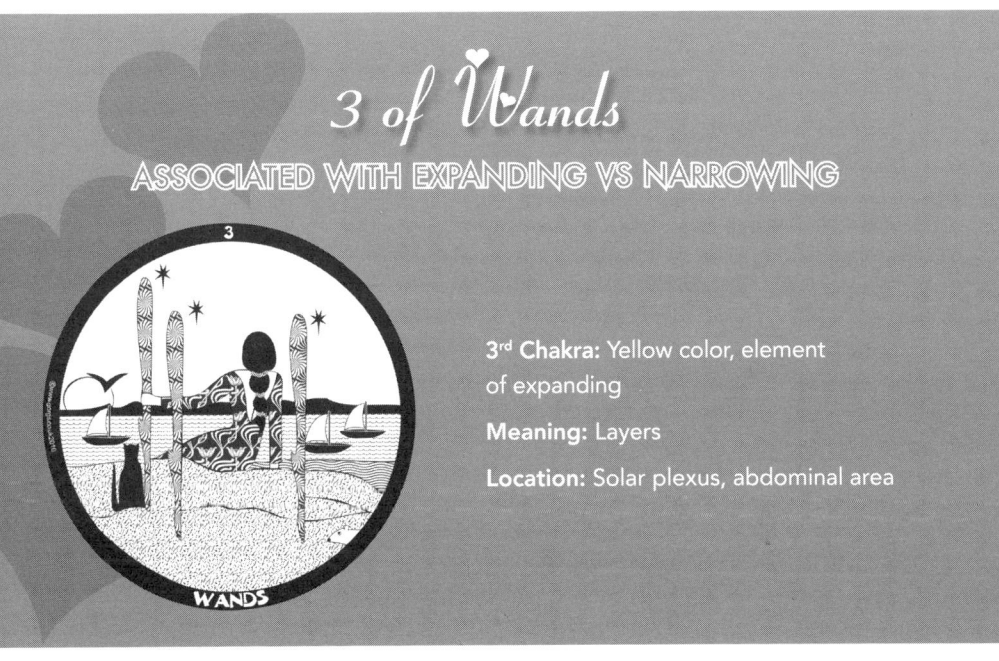

3 of Wands
ASSOCIATED WITH EXPANDING VS NARROWING

3rd Chakra: Yellow color, element of expanding

Meaning: Layers

Location: Solar plexus, abdominal area

A fulfillment of satisfaction is felt in this relationship, along with working hard at what works for both you and your partner. There are three layers that work in developing a long-standing relationship: cooperation with one another, consideration, and understanding. Cooperation can elevate self-absorbed issues one may be feeling towards their partner, allowing understanding of what is expected. Also, roles in the relationship can cut down on arguments, and help with understanding both views. Cooperation creates harmony in the relationship by working hand-in-hand together to make it work; for example, one cooks and the other does the dishes. Consideration enables one to have awareness of the partner's circumstances or thoughts and draws your attention to the situation. One may have a headache, so the other turns the TV volume to low. Understanding has both partners relating to each other's needs. One may be so tired from the day, that the other relates to the tiredness and takes the trash out for them.

METAPHORICAL

Cooking with a partner in the kitchen who helps boil the cooking water, cut up the meat, and set the table enables the task to flow with continuity and creates an enjoyable experience.

GENERAL MEANING FOR 3 OF WANDS

- Opportunity, overconfidence, manipulation for one's gain
- New job offer, living in a new country, positive outcome for any application process
- Travel over water, satisfaction, waiting and knowing good things are arriving soon

QUESTION STATEMENT:
How do you express your consideration and understating to your partner?

AFFIRMATION:
I'm aware of how I express my thoughts and emotions to my partner.

TIMING:
3 days, 3 weeks, 3 months, 3rd day of the week, March 21-April 20

3 of Pentacles
ASSOCIATED WITH ACQUIRE VS DENY

3rd Chakra: Yellow color, element of expressing opinion

Meaning: Lack of emotion in the relationship

Location: Solar plexus, abdominal area

Working together and forming a life has been the foundation in this relationship. Both parties have been working towards similar goals: family, career, and home.

With busy lifestyles and attention to goals, the emotional expression to one another may have been forgotten. Expressing emotions in a relationship enables each partner to feel what the other feels through physical touch, verbal communication, and action. Embracing one another in the morning before heading off to begin the day is a good way to start. In the evening, a simple smile or compliment is another way to express how one feels. One partner may be more repressed in their expression of feelings then the other; this can be because of personality, like traits of an earth sign (Taurus, Capricorn, or Virgo). Both of you are able to work with each other in daily activities without arguments.

METAPHORICAL

Expressing an emotion like anger or a feeling of unhappiness is not that easy for everyone to communicate to their partner. Withholding one's feelings and not talking about it allows one to suppress their nature. If someone cuts in front of you while driving on the highway, do you yell and press on your horn or do you ignore the action?

GENERAL MEANING FOR THE 3 OF PENTACLES

- Getting a job promotion or a job, pregnancy, birth, adoption, not working hard enough
- Stomach or colon problems, good outcome in any transactions, staying focused
- Making improvements with an issue, socialite, materialism

QUESTION STATEMENT:
Do you have an emotionless relationship?

AFFIRMATION:
I enjoy telling my partner that I love him or her.

TIMING:
3 days, 3 weeks, 3 months, 3rd day of the week, December 21-January 20

4 of Cups
ASSOCIATED WITH DISAFFECTION VS CONTENTEDNESS

4th Chakra: Color green or pink, element of desire

Meaning: Not accepting what is being offered

Location: Chest area

One may be withholding emotions from their partner, not really expressing how they feel. Whether its sadness, fear, or happiness, they are keeping it within. This has nothing to do with you as the partner or what you are doing in the relationship. You may have noticed that your partner is withdrawing and behaving more like an introvert. This is the result of the lack of fulfillment in their own personal life, a feeling of unhappiness – like their career, or more specifically, a desire to want more out of a career. Also, the lack of career fulfillment leads them to a restless state that hinders their judgment and the way they treat you. Too, they may have had a relationship in the past that has made them feel like a failure.

The inability to talk about what's going on internally with their feelings propels them to act out in a self-destructive manner, whether it's talking to other people, looking for fast flings to fulfill that unsatisfactory feeling created by the restlessness, or eating or spending too much on themselves. Things will improve for your partner's career; this will allow them to feel more stable within themselves. A personality of keeping things inside can be due to an astrological sign or their upbringing and cultural environment. Looking at the situation that created the problem will allow a different perspective and possible new outcomes.

METAPHORICAL

This could be called the white-picket-fence syndrome. Growing up, one dreams of owning a house with a white picket fence. When finally an adult and owner of a house of their dreams, there still may be feelings of discontent if they do not feel what they thought they would by owning the dream house.

GENERAL MEANING FOR 4 OF CUPS

- One feeling disconnected with life, not seeing other opportunities
- Dissatisfaction with life, confusion that creates procrastination
- Depressed, feeling that one has lost new opportunities

QUESTION STATEMENT:
Do you take it personal when things don't go right with your partner?
How do you encourage them?

AFFIRMATION:
I own my emotions and feelings.

TIMING:
4 days, 4 weeks, 4 months, 4th day of the week, June 22-July 22

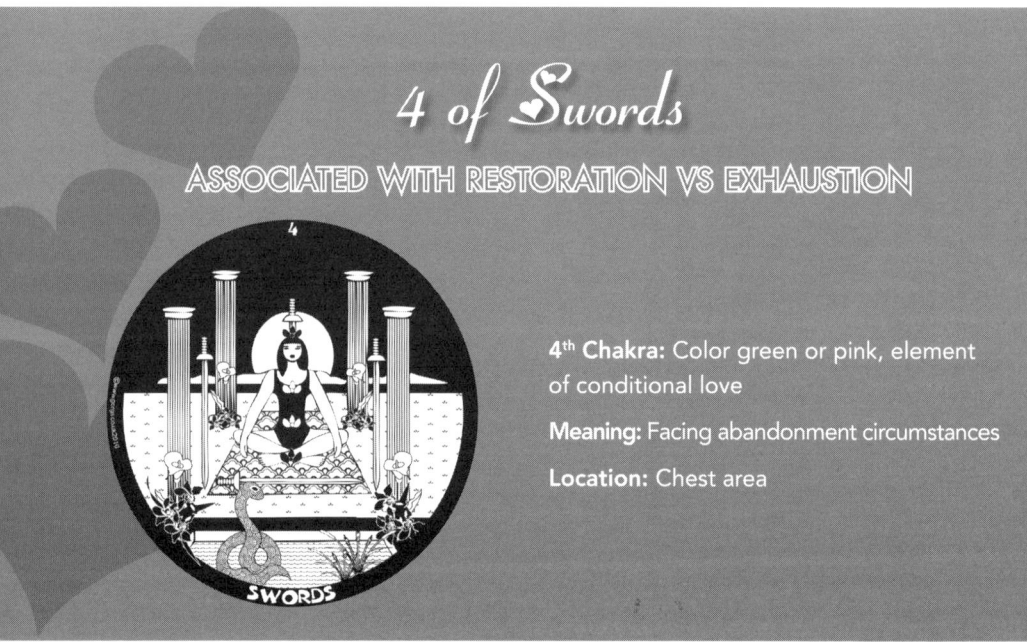

4 of Swords
ASSOCIATED WITH RESTORATION VS EXHAUSTION

4th Chakra: Color green or pink, element of conditional love

Meaning: Facing abandonment circumstances

Location: Chest area

Your relationship may have felt that it was in a stagnate period. Know that things are improving, as you and your partner were able to work out an agreement and come to peace with whatever issues that had to be dealt with. Four elements that have worked in this relationship are forgiveness, love, acceptance, and surrender. This happened because partners were able to listen without interruptions and judgments. Understanding was created, enabling the relationship to push forth any issues needing to be worked through. The Four Rs – relax, rejuvenate, reverence, and resurrection – are important.

METAPHORICAL

Playing the childhood game of cops and robbers, one is tied up in the handcuffs and made immobile. Then the key unlocks the cuffs, allowing freedom.

GENERAL MEANING FOR 4 OF SWORDS

- Calling a truce, facing past issues with a relative, gaining clarity for an issue
- Rest needed, family visit involving traveling, a person that secludes themselves
- Death/resurrection, feeling abandon, meditation to gain insight and alleviate stress
- Vacation plans, protecting one's feelings from being hurt, emotional cleansing

Question statement:
What are some issues where you and your partner were able to call a truce?

Affirmation:
As I breathe in positive air, I exhale negative feelings.

Timing:
4 days, 4 weeks, 4 months, 4th day of the week, September 23-October 23

4 of Wands
ASSOCIATED WITH REINFORCE VS LESSEN

4th Chakra: Color green or pink, element of compassion

Meaning: Living together

Location: Chest area

This is a time to harmonize in the relationship. Both parties are in a place where they want and seek the same things. Whether it's living together or an engagement, marriage, or moving-in situation, both are in accordance in making things work. Events may not happen as quickly as you would like to see them manifest, but the intention of both partners is to make the relationship work. The Four Cs are involved: creativity, communication, careful, and considerate (with each other). Participation with one another enabled both parties to build towards a common goal. For example, both parties participated in communication, staying in tune with each other and asking and receiving insight into each other's daily lives. It may have been as simple as asking: How was your day? How are you feeling? You may have greeted each other with a warm embrace, a massage for tired feet, or you may have set time aside for one another on a weekly basis to reconnect.

Also, one may be in the process of decorating or renovating the house. If this is a new relationship, it's off to a great start.

METAPHORICAL

The creativity, style of furniture, and amenities of a house make it cozy and warm. When one of these elements is missing, it affects the energy of the home.

GENERAL MEANING FOR 4 OF WANDS

- Love, jealousy, moving in together, graduation
- Trust, envy, long-distance relationship, going on vacation
- Compassion, moving on, easily irritated, worked hard and now enjoying the benefits

Question statement:
What's one piece of advice you can give someone who is missing what you have in your relationship?

Affirmation:
I love my house; my house loves me.

Timing:
4 days, 4 weeks, 4 months, 4th day of the week, March 21-April 19

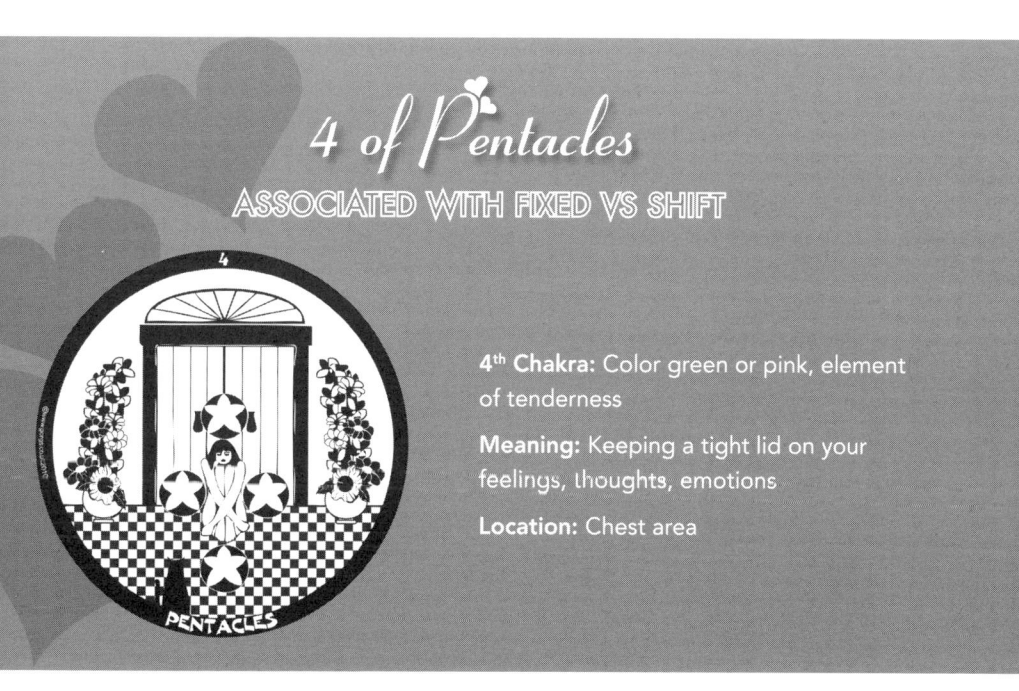

4 of Pentacles
ASSOCIATED WITH FIXED VS SHIFT

4th Chakra: Color green or pink, element of tenderness

Meaning: Keeping a tight lid on your feelings, thoughts, emotions

Location: Chest area

Maintaining what is currently going on in your relationship, no changes, and equilibrium. One may not be so expressive with their affection, whether it's hugs, kisses, or holding hands. The repression of the physical attention can cause the other partner to feel frustrated, insecure, and confused. The partner tends to keep even mundane things to themselves, whether they are good or bad. The repressed partner stays in the relationship because they're looking at it as a possible future gain, so little emotions are focused within them. The stinginess with their expression of feelings and affection creates a controlling and smothering situation and they push around their partner.

There are no losses in your relationship financially and no big gains. You're able to keep "financial balance," and you're in a good place. What you make financially covers your expenses and you're not feeling a significant loss in your budget. This card does indicate possibly a partner who looks at his or her career as a financial gain involving their social status, and looks to assist you in your career in a way that can be pushy or even controlling – holding on tight.

You have had ups and downs in this relationship, but know it's stable. This gives you the opportunity to think about what the next chapter will be, whether it's buying a house, adding a family member, or other considerations. It gives you the time to pause and rejuvenate.

Metaphorical

Going to the museum, like the Smithsonian Institute, is a great experience – seeing all the incredible artifacts. You can look, but not touch. In a relationship, you may have the partner, but you may not *feel* that you do (i.e., jealousy may play a part).

GENERAL MEANING FOR 4 OF PENTACLES

- Maintains the status of what you have, looking at material success, controlling personality
- A child who acts like an adult, imbalance of emotions that creates suffocation
- Good outcome for any application process, someone coming from wealth, jealousy, divorce
- Comes from a divorced background, a jealous partner who doesn't want their mate to have friends

Question statement:
When was the last time your partner hugged you?

Affirmation:
I love expressing how I feel to my partner and vice versa.

Timing:
4 days, 4 weeks, 4 months, 4th day of the week, December 22-January 19

5 of Cups
ASSOCIATED WITH NONINVOLVEMENT VS INVOLVEMENT

5th Chakra: Color blue, element of thought
Meaning: Disconnection with self
Location: Throat

This card indicates a partner dealing with losing the connection with themselves and causing a self-indulgent behavior that aids in numbing their feelings. They may have started out with an arrogant personality; then, with things going differently, life chipped away at them until their self-centered ideas and entitled thinking were broken down. They may have acted impulsively at times and had a personality as a know-it-all, just like a narcissus.

In the relationship, you may be feeling that your partner is turning away and trying still to succeed with the loss of their self connection, making you ask the questions: Where are you? Where are we in this relationship? Wanting more than they have, and not getting it, causes them to turn feelings into anger or aggression inside.

METAPHORICAL

Going snorkeling is relaxing, but trying to paddle at the shore line doesn't allow one to connect to the reef to see the view.

GENERAL MEANING FOR 5 OF CUPS

- Turning your back on certain things in order to succeed, secretive with problems
- Drinking too much, the need to overcome problems
- Walking away from an unfinished situation, needs clarity of a situation
- Delays in any financial or business transactions, miscarriage

QUESTION STATEMENT:
What part of your life is unfulfilled?

AFFIRMATION:
I'm excited about all the opportunities that life presents me.

TIMING:
5 days, Thursday, 5th month, 5 weeks, October 24-November 21

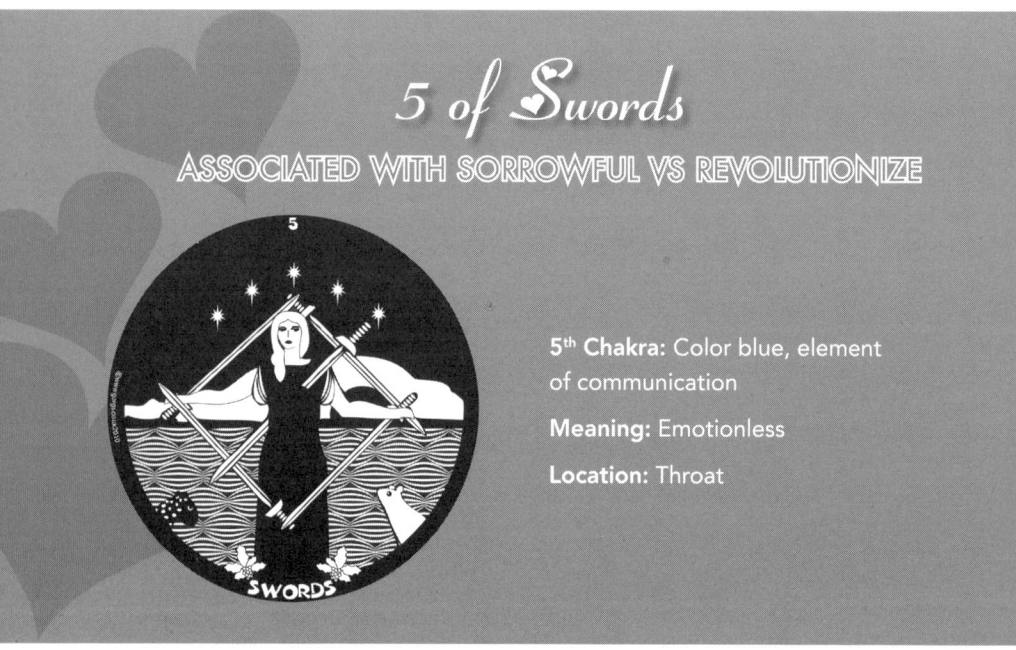

5 of Swords
ASSOCIATED WITH SORROWFUL VS REVOLUTIONIZE

5th Chakra: Color blue, element of communication

Meaning: Emotionless

Location: Throat

Detachment in the relationship can create healthy, emotional boundaries and allow the other person to be who they are, without one partner controlling the other, such as dictating how one should act, what clothes to wear, what job to take, how much money to make, or the way to speak. This also includes taking charge of their own actions and responsibilities for the choices they make, not being a rescuer by trying to clean up the mistakes that the partner makes. Having a lack of emotional boundaries leaves one feeling defeated and lowers self-esteem, which causes loss of independence. Taking responsibility for your own actions and feelings is an example of a healthy part of your emotional boundaries, as well as not blaming or projecting one's mistakes on someone or something else. This gives the relationship a stronger platform and doesn't leave one feeling that their partner is unpredictable in conversation or situations.

Metaphorical

A sergeant in the army gives orders and demands discipline. There is no back talk to the sergeant because his or her job is to train and see that soldiers follow orders.

GENERAL MEANING FOR THE 5 OF SWORDS

- Trying to control someone's behavior, attention to taking care of personal needs
- Manipulation for personal gain, sleight of hand, self destruction/out of control
- Trying to play the fixer in the relationship, ignoring feelings, feeling uncertain about finances
- Intimidating environment, addictions for masking hidden issues, regret of a past action
- An egotistical person who spreads gossip, backstabbing, personality clashes

Question statement:
How would you define the emotional boundaries in your relationship?

Affirmation:
I'm responsible for my emotions, and I feel good about it.

Timing:
5 days, Thursday, 5th month, 5 weeks, January 20-February 18

5 of Wands
ASSOCIATED WITH BOASTFULNESS VS HUMILITY

5th Chakra: Color blue, element of responsibility

Meaning: Competition in a competitive environment

Location: Throat

Great team work; partners may compete with each other, work in the same field, and work well together, always giving a helping hand. You and your partner can be argumentative with each other, however, and both of you have a strong personality. When you express a thought or comment, it goes straight over your partner's head and vice versus. This can lead to difficulty getting points across. It's good to work on different techniques of communication so you won't wear each other out. Learn to pick what's worth arguing about and let your partner be right sometimes. It's not about being right all the time. It's not worth a fight in the relationship – you are partners, not enemies. The competition between the two of you might feel like that sometimes. As mentioned, both of you have strong presence in personality, and go well with each other. There may be one thing your partner wants you to change, and hopes that you do, but that's just the partner's strong point of view coming out. In time, both of you will learn to respect each other for what you are – or part ways as friends.

You may feel restricted in your home environment with your partner when communicating; this causes frustration and arguments. The way thoughts and emotions are expressed in this relationship have limitation due to both partners' egos. Setting boundaries regarding how to have a conversation (like listening, then pausing for five seconds before responding) will allow the other partner to be heard, and vice versa.

Metaphorical

Playing chess requires a strategy of not only what a partner's next move will be, but also what one's own move will be. It requires thinking and a plan.

GENERAL MEANING FOR 5 OF WANDS

- Competing for a job, internal frustration, situation that pushes you
- Arguing and your point of view not heard, feeling restricted, ambitious, outburst of emotions
- Someone who loves sports, manipulative personality, sexual, high maintenance

Question Statement:
When you and your partner talk,
are you focused on getting your point of view heard?
How about your partner?

Affirmation:
When I speak, I speak to listen.

Timing:
5 days, Thursday, 5th month, 5 weeks, July 23-August 22

5 of Pentacles
ASSOCIATED WITH CLOSED VS OPEN

5th Chakra: Color blue, element of security
Meaning: Inability to express your thoughts
Location: Throat

Not speaking how one really feels can lead to being left out for certain opportunities to change the dynamic in the relationship and this is by their choice, their own inability to speak up. Your partner may not see your view, though. But at the end, it works out very well for you, and just what you thought the outcome should be is what comes to be. There is something in the relationship that needs to be said; however, one partner in the relationship doesn't feel like they can express what they want to say to the other. It's important to talk about what is on your mind. If there is anything that you want to express to your partner and you have been withholding, now it is the time to speak.

Someone may be reflecting about a past relationship and have regrets regarding how things turned out. Now that person is in the position of watching the ex move on into a more emotional, fulfilled relationship, as they stand on the outside looking in at the ex's new relationship. There is a desire by an ex to speak to their prior partner to clear out old wounds and to apologize for how behaviors were handled towards the end of the relationship.

METAPHORICAL

A man tells his partner that he will be back and is only going to the store to buy some milk – and never returns. The women never was able to express how she felt and the man never gave closure to the relationship.

GENERAL MEANING FOR 5 OF PENTACLES

- Overlooking details that can cause an error
- An ex with a meddling in-law, one feeling left out and unable to speak up

QUESTION STATEMENT:
Is there anything that you would like to express to your partner that you're holding back?

AFFIRMATION:
I'm a beautiful person, and I love this beautiful life.

TIMING:
5 days, Thursday, 5th month, 5 weeks, April 20-May 20

6 of Cups
ASSOCIATED WITH LONGING VS INVOLVEMENT

6th Chakra: Color indigo, element of the inner child

Meaning: Attachment to family

Location: 3rd eye, mid brain

There is a deep sense of passion between you and your partner. One may even be obsessing to see how the other feels. Your partner may have a curious and carefree attitude. Also, one may feel that something is missing from the relationship that they yearn for. They may have grown up in a household where they were used to having a certain behavior, and now, being in this relationship, that behavior is missing. The behavior can be anything from affection and expressing one's thoughts to having someone make their bed, etc. You and your partner may share something in common from the past childhood; it can be anything from celebrating the holidays in the same way to having similar parental upbringing. One has to look at their inner child and how that has an effect on the relationship. Was one spoiled as a child and now feels a sense of entitlement? Was there abuse, which has led to self-abandoning issues, like drinking or promiscuity? The way one's emotional and childhood upbringing and memories surface affect who they are today. There may be a need to play more in your relationship.

METAPHORICAL

Playing kick ball in life can represent what opportunities life kicks towards you and your ability to have fun in the process.

GENERAL MEANING FORF 6 OF CUPS

- An unexpected job opportunity, immature, opportunities from past efforts
- A person who engages in one-night stands, having fun in relationships, unconditional love
- Childhood memories, thinking of the past and missing how things were

QUESTION STATEMENT:
When was the last time you and your partner played together?
(Board games, tag, etc.)

AFFIRMATION:
I enjoy playing; it makes me feel joyous.

TIMING:
6 days, 6th month, 6 weeks, Saturday, October 24-November 21

6 of Swords
ASSOCIATED WITH ORIGINAL VS CHANGE

6th Chakra: Color indigo, element of awakening

Meaning: Flow of the river

Location: 3rd eye, mid-brain

The intellect between partners is similar. Partners share a similar career and like to hear each other's point of view. One may be traveling alone to see their partner over or near water; this is a better period in your relationship. Both have experienced up and downs – even doubting if the relationship will work out – but know it is headed for better times, including finances, housing, or planning for a family. Going through the rough spots has carved out a direction showing where they're headed and how being together makes them happy. The relationship will still need some work, but both are coming into a more stable period. The desire for travel comes to play with both partners; one or both may like to travel more, whether it's just for fun, business, or family obligations. One person(s) has a natural need to change environments, which adds freshness to their personality with regards to how they deal with their partner. A getaway weekend can add rejuvenation. Also, one may have mixed emotions: one day feeling detached and unemotional, and the next day being friendly and engaging.

METAPHORICAL

White water rafting is an amazing experience. You hit rough patches of water while in the kayak, but then there is also smooth sailing ahead – both allow one to enjoy the experience.

GENERAL MEANING FOR 6 OF SWORDS

- Expression, unemotional person, traveling to see your partner
- Intellectual, a friendly situation, getting a job in another country
- Curiosity, reveals problems that need to be overcome

QUESTION STATEMENT:
What direction is your relationship headed?

AFFIRMATION:
Obstacles give me a chance to build my character.

TIMING:
6 days, 6th month, 6 weeks, Saturday, January 20-February 18

6 of Wands
ASSOCIATED WITH FOCUS VS HAZY

6th Chakra: Color indigo, element of being centered

Meaning: Center of attention, people watching

Location: 3rd eye, mid-brain

The relationship has reached a point of mutual contentment. You and your partner may be spending a lot of time out socializing, whether it's for work or personal enjoyment. The awareness of the behavior between partners has reached a conscious level. You both are aware how each treats the other, respecting each other's conversations, wishes, and decisions. Both mirror behavior. One may be very gregarious in affection with their partner; however, though the partner enjoys the affection, he or she is not comfortable in expressing or receiving this type of care. Or, one may be feeling like their behaviors or actions are being watched – this can make one of the partners feel like there is a need to keep up an "ideal look" regarding what a relationship should be or be cognizant of what is expected from others. The attraction between the partners is mutual: good-looking partners making a picture-perfect couple. There is success in both partners' careers.

METAPHORICAL

Performing in a play or being part of a parade has the person involved as the center of attention. Aware of being at the center of attention and the enjoyment it provides, the crowd reciprocates.

GENERAL MEANING FOR 6 OF WANDS

- Success in finances, anything to do with papers, a desire to want more out of life
- Achievement in education, who you surround yourself with has an effect
- A good outcome regardless of the doubt, intuitive sense of what is to come

QUESTION STATEMENT:
What would your advice be for a successful relationship?

AFFIRMATION:
I'm thankful for all my continuous success.

TIMING:
6 days, 6th month, 6 weeks, Saturday, July 23-August 22

6th Chakra: Color indigo, element of clarity
Meaning: Being fair
Location: 3rd eye, mid-brain

Equality of feelings is represented in this card. Financially, when one makes more income than the other in a relationship, or is even more intellectual or insightful, this is not felt or expressed by the other partner. The person's ego is not driven here, allowing for comfortable interactions between the two. Also, when decisions need to be made, fairness in the relationship is front and center. One partner doesn't make the other feel less significant. There is an emotional stability among partners, both helping each other to succeed in life. If there are dependency issues, this will only be temporary, until one moves on their way to a new job or position.

Metaphorical

Growing up with a sibling, chores were shared, such as sweeping the floor and getting paid the same amount of money no matter who did what; there was fairness.

GENERAL MEANING FOR 6 OF PENTACLES

- Financial payment given, something given or being offered that you like
- Receiving a yes answer to selling, buying, or receiving a loan, improved situation
- Debts paid, a promotional opportunity

Question statement:
What is you method of success for treating your partner equally?

Affirmation:
I'm grateful for all the success I have in my life.

Timing:
6 days, 6th month, 6 weeks, Saturday, April 20-May 20

7 of Cups
ASSOCIATED WITH ILLUSIONARY OPTION VS UNREACHABLE

7th Chakra: All colors (white), or violet, gold, element of conscious choice

Meaning: Is this it?

Location: Above the head, crown area

Strong emotions are expressed in this relationship, like how one feels sexually within the partnership – one may be acting out of jealousy, with manipulative talk. Not everything that goes on in the relationship is talked about, though. With the emotions of one partner combined with the sexual energy that they hold together, a combustion of confusion is created – confusion, because one has the deep desire and the want to be intimate, but also wants to have alone time. So, balancing is the key. Also, one can get caught up with how something will feel or be, but once they reach the desired point, they then realize that it's completely different from their idea or thought. There, too, may be confusion about where to go in the relationship.

METAPHORICAL

You've gotten the dream job that you went to school for, but then wonder: Is this it? The expectation is not what you initially felt about that sought-after position.

GENERAL MEANING FOR 7 OF CUPS

- Confusion about what choice to make, someone being secretive
- Daydreamers, the seduction of superficial flings
- A lot of choices and options, buying/shopping for things for psychological needs

QUESTION STATEMENT:
After working towards a goal and accomplishing what you set out to do, what was your initial reaction and why?

AFFIRMATION:
I appreciate what I have accomplished.

TIMING:
7 days, 7th month, 7 weeks, Sunday, October 24-November 21

7 of Swords
ASSOCIATED WITH MOTIONLESS VS STIMULATING

7th Chakra: All colors (white), or violet, gold, element of mental and emotional action

Meaning: Unpredictable events that change plans

Location: Above the head, crown area

There is a feeling of a stagnation period; the relationship has not reached a level the couple had hoped for. There was goal to reach a certain point, but that has yet to come to pass. This could include anything from a marriage or proposal to a divorce to start and end, or a new job that changes the career path and brings a move. One may be feeling the inability to express how they feel or what they want to happen in the situation because of what their partner may be thinking or how it will be interpreted.

METAPHORICAL

It is shocking and disappointing to find out that one of your closest friends has spoken badly about you and is not trustworthy; for example, going for the same job as a friend and then this friend sabotages your opportunity for the job.

GENERAL MEANING FOR 7 OF SWORDS

- New plans due to backstabbing, trusting the wrong people
- Your confidence gives you new opportunities, financial gain
- Living by water, not getting the first job offer, but the second one

Question statement:
When was the last time you listened to your gut feeling?

Affirmation:
I trust my instincts and intuition.

Timing:
7 days, 7th month, 7 weeks, Sunday, January 20-February 18

ASSOCIATED WITH UNWAVERING VS HESITANT

7th Chakra: All colors (white), or violet, gold, element of action

Meaning: Number one employee

Location: Above the head, crown area

Both you and your partner are interested in what is going on with each other's career growth and how it is affecting your home environment. There has been a challenge in the past, but the two of you were able to forge through and work out the difficulties with the causes of conflict, whether it was changing jobs, or moving. Both know where each other stands in the relationship, meaning the position and how a role is played. One can be the nurturer, the listener, or the provider. There are many roles that are played, and who plays what part depends on the circumstances. Both partners are self-sufficient and independent in making choices.

METAPHORICAL

Think of standing on a stack of logs and still keeping one's balance. Not only are the logs sturdy, but the balance is at the right point of origin, so it gives one the ability to stand tall.

GENERAL MEANING FOR 7 OF WANDS

- Decisions that need to be made that may come off as inconsiderate
- Actions that need to be taken, success in a competition
- Receiving a desired outcome, staying on top of any situation
- Getting a job that requires a change, vocal personality

QUESTION STATEMENT:
When was the last time your partner was trying to compete with you?

AFFIRMATION:
I respect other people's views, even though I have different ones.

TIMING:
7 days, 7th month, 7 weeks, Sunday, July 23-August 22

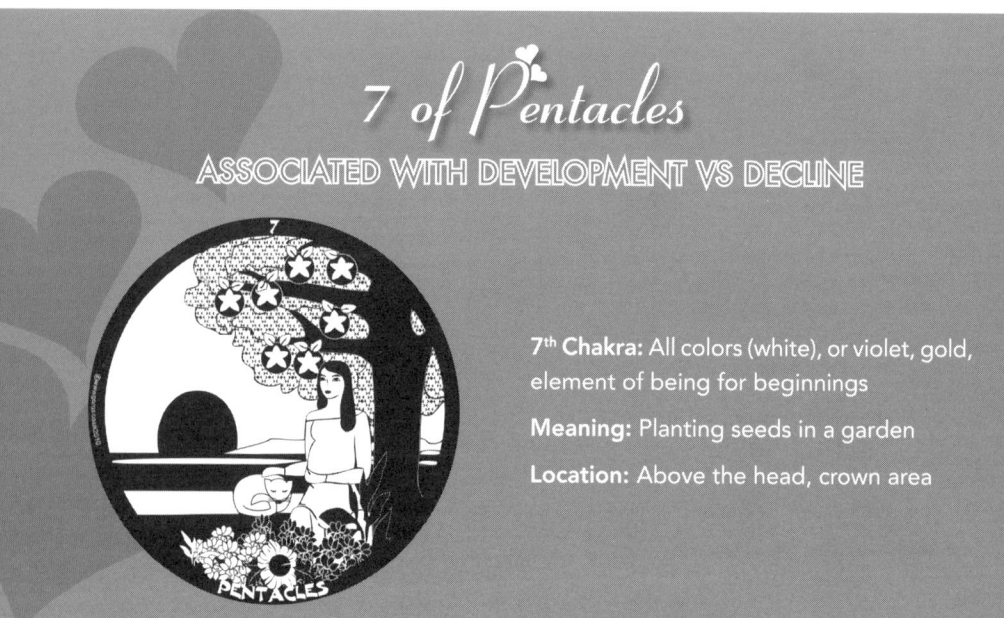

7 of Pentacles
ASSOCIATED WITH DEVELOPMENT VS DECLINE

7th Chakra: All colors (white), or violet, gold, element of being for beginnings

Meaning: Planting seeds in a garden

Location: Above the head, crown area

As the relationship begins and continues to grow, limited possibilities are created regarding where you and your partner can take it. Could marriage or children be right for the partnership or should you work together? Now is the time to be clear about your boundaries and where you would like to see the relationship go. This will help the formation of a healthy and caring relationship. Otherwise, stress and anxiety can have an effect on one's health, like headaches or depression. The relationship may have taken some time to get to a place where one would like to see it, whether it's financial or feeling connected to a partner or marriage. This leaves one feeling uncertain in how things will turn out and if they will develop in the way the one has in mind.

Metaphorical

Planting flowers or a garden is a relaxing and creative thing to do. Watering them and adding fertilizer is needed for the growth of the seeds.

General Meaning for 7 of Pentacles

- Prosperity, having determination in a situation
- Self discipline, working on a project that will take time to show results
- Boundaries, depression caused by being impatient
- Birth, growing, planting ideas, something that is done that involves risk, but also security

Question statement:
What kind of seeds (expression) do you feed into your relationship?

Affirmation:
I appreciate my partner in my life and what we have been able to grow together.

Timing:
7 days, 7th month, 7 weeks, Sunday, fall, April 20-May 20

8 of Cups
ASSOCIATED WITH TODAY VS TOMORROW

4th Chakra: Color green, element of rejecting or accepting

Meaning: 1 Lunar Cycle

Location: Chest area

This card shows how one takes actions in a relationship. A decision is indicated that will move the relationship in a new direction – a change for the better. It can mean that, in one month's time, a decision that needs to be implemented in the relationship is likely to happen. There may be emotional issues involved that could cause your partner to walk away or need a break, or you or your partner may have decided that the relationship isn't going to work. This can also indicate that there may be a change in the partner's behavior because of an inability to complete what they'd set out to do. The lack of attention in their daily life is causing them anguish. They may not have enough confidence within about their own abilities, or they may not know how to start and finish reaching the goals that they'd set for themselves, so they project discontent onto the partner or vice versa.

METAPHORICAL

Waking up in the morning brings a new day and a fresh start, which allows one to begin on a new path. A new day gives new experiences and chances.

GENERAL MEANING FOR 8 OF CUPS

- Change in plans brought on by a positive decision
- Stressful circumstances

QUESTION STATEMENT:
What recent changes have been made in your relationship? How did you feel about it?

AFFIRMATION:
I have control of my emotions and express them with love and respect for others.

TIMING:
8 days, 8 weeks, 8 months, August, February 19-March 20

8 of Swords
ASSOCIATED WITH REPETITIVE VS FRAGMENT

4th Chakra: Color green, element of complex emotional patterns

Meaning: Mixed Emotions

Location: Chest area

Swords are one of the four building blocks of a relationship, which represents communication, expression, and connection. When 8 of Swords appears in a relationship reading, this can indicate that you or your partner feel like they are repeating or they are finding themselves in the same behavior pattern. The partner may be too critical of you or nitpicking, or you may be treating your partner in that way. You may find yourself picking the same type of partners for a relationship: Did you pick this relationship just so you would not be alone, or were you or your partner suppressing an empty heart from a previous relationship? Partners may feel locked in the relationship based on psychological needs. This locked feeling is not psychical, but difficult to walk away from (maybe due to low self-esteem or not enough confidence in one's ability). You or your partner may find fault with the relationship or blame others for the current situation. One of you may be controlling. Or, you or your partner may not show emotions or be as affectionate as the other would like. One may be an introvert and the other an extrovert, so the differences may cause compromise. At the beginning of the relationship, you or your partner may have been blinded by the other's beauty, or because of the attraction, someone failed to see the real person in front of them. Also, you or your partner may want to end the relationship, but later, have second thoughts. This card can additionally indicate that you or your partner stay in this relationship for fear of being alone. Not getting emotional needs met by the partner, the "communication effectiveness" needs to be worked on – what one partner is giving is what he or she most likely wants back, and is not getting. For example, one partner may be very affectionate towards their partner, yet the partner is not affectionate in return; this has a tendency to create anger and disconnection. Teamwork needs to be applied – it cannot be his or her way alone. Say to yourself: *What's good for my partner is good for me.*

METAPHORICAL

There may be a goal set in mind to lose weight, but every day you repeat the same behavioral patterns that sabotage your success in weight loss. Reverse this pattern by first, forgiving yourself for not being perfect. Next, set up fire extinguishers to put a halt on temptation, whether it's cookies, candy, or eating over your target caloric intake. Third, carry around in-between-meal snacks, like fruit, yogurt, or nuts. Then increase your daily activity level; for instance, take a walk, or walk the dog, or, go back to the gym.

GENERAL MEANING FOR 8 OF SWORDS

- Restriction stipulations limits conditions, control, not able to control temptations
- Limitations, criticizing, finding fault, blame, disapproval brings low self-esteem issues
- Repeating the same behavioral pattern

QUESTION STATEMENT:
What cycle or patterns do you find yourself in?
What patterns does your partner have in the relationship?
What is one step or action you can take to break the cycle?

AFFIRMATION:
I will not let my old patterns be part of my future.

TIMING:
8 days, 8 weeks, the month of August, or 2 months, May 21-June 21

8 of Wands
ASSOCIATED WITH GRAVITATION VS REPEL

4th Chakra: Color green, element of movement

Meaning: Part of a building block

Location: Chest area

The 8 of Wands shows an element of creativity used in forming a foundation, which is unionship, companionship, or the family unit of a relationship. It's like looking at building and seeing what the building is made of – cement, wood, rocks, etc. When 8 of Wands is in a Tarot reading, this can depict that the creativity or imagined plans or wants of the relationship are not going where you or your partner would like, or thought, they would go. The beginning of the relationship was quick, or you may have met your significant other unexpectedly and ended up in a fast love affair, only to find out later that any future progress was being delayed. Delay can cause friction or arguments, as well as a lack of partner motivation in finishing something up in his or her personal life so that the current relationship can move forward. This can include, as example, finalizing or setting a date for marriage, or finishing anything that has to do with documents, paperwork, or a signature (whether it is used for buying a house or car, getting a divorce, signing the divorce papers, filing for immigration, or meeting the future in-laws, etc.). Lack of motivation in these areas can lead to disagreements, but these issues are solvable once you or your partner makes the committed effort to complete the needed details and move forward. Also, you or your partner may have hang ups and use these as excuses to move forward. One or the other may have a fiery personality, which may be quick to flare.

Metaphorical

When shooting a bow and arrow, the arrows are shot up into the sky. All the creative energy (love in the relationship) goes up; then, with time, the arrows fall back down to the ground due to gravity (the planes in the relationship).

GENERAL MEANING FOR 8 OF WANDS

- Creativity, action/non-action, causing agreements, swiftness
- Flying, delayed flying, hasty, careful
- Sudden, gradual, rapid, unexpected sluggishness
- Wanting the relationship to be in another place than where it is currently

Question Statement:
What is holding back your relationship? Why?
What is one thing that you can communicate to your partner to enhance the movement of the relationship forward?
What is the reason for you or your partner not taking the necessary steps to move forward?

Affirmation:
I am aware of what is blocking the progression of my relationship, and I am taking responsibility for my actions.

Timing:
8 days, weeks, May 21-June 21

8 of Pentacles
ASSOCIATED WITH METICULOUS VS VAGUE

4th Chakra: Color green, element of rejecting or accepting

Meaning: Using a hammer and nails

Location: Chest area

This card indicates work and paying attention to details in the relationship. You may be involved with a conservative person, or feel like your partner is narrow-minded or stubborn. The personality related here isn't a risk taker, but there is an opportunity to work on the relationship and to go for another positive chance. Also, someone may be seeking help, i.e., from an advisor, coach, or therapist. Both partners are working at the relationship, having that feeling of being on the same level. The relationship has improved over the time you and your partner have been together. Additionally, you or your partner may be hard at work at a chosen craft/job; it seems that the days are filled with your partner gone and working. The job may give your partner a sense of satisfaction and purpose. The partners may be working on the same issues before getting it right and making the relationship closer.

METAPHORICAL

Crafting with wood takes detail and precision for the desired and accurate appearance that makes the wood carvers decal so special and one of a kind.

GENERAL MEANING FOR 8 OF PENTACLES

- Employment opportunity
- Being Alone

QUESTION STATEMENT:
Do you feel like your partner or you focus too much on the same issue?

AFFIRMATION:
Before I criticize, I think about how that will affect the other person.

TIMING:
8 days, 8 weeks, 8 months, August 23-September 22

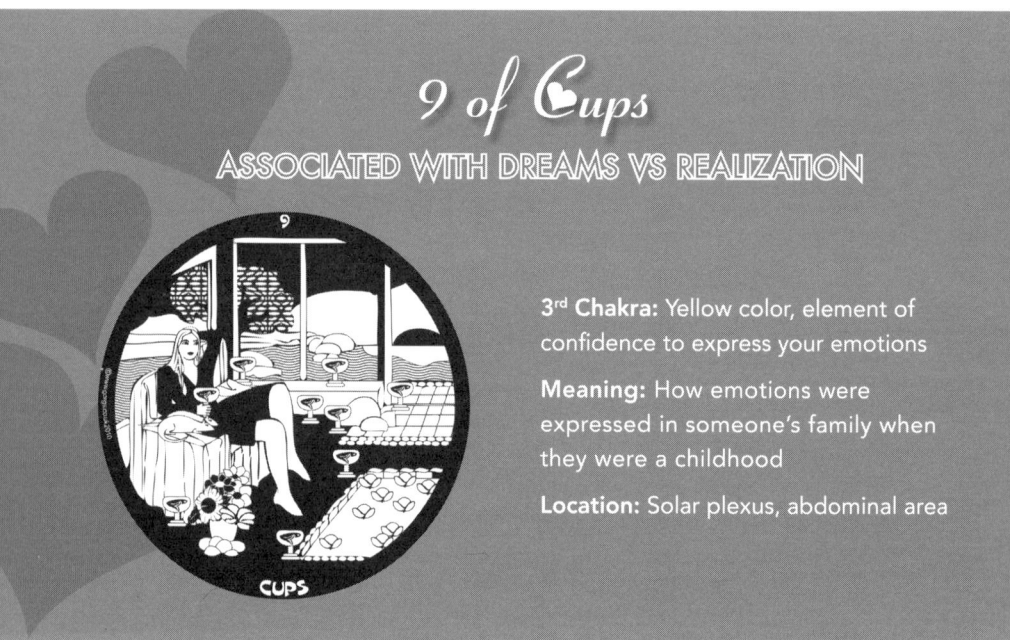

9 of Cups
ASSOCIATED WITH DREAMS VS REALIZATION

3rd Chakra: Yellow color, element of confidence to express your emotions

Meaning: How emotions were expressed in someone's family when they were a childhood

Location: Solar plexus, abdominal area

Desires and a feeling of gratification is felt in this relationship. Partners feel how much love they both have towards one another; also, there is a supporting environment with each partner's individual goals taken into consideration. There is satisfaction in the way the partners express their love and appreciation for each other, whether it's hugging, holding hands, or talking openly about their views in life. This card signifies getting what you desire in a relationship – it's emotionally fulfilling and headed in a positive direction. Emotional fulfillment occurs as time progresses in the relationship; this is due to learning that, in the past, unsatisfied relationships did not provide a supportive environment. One may be left feeling withdrawn and depressed from negative communication. This can be a catalyst for divorce and cheating. The relationship could have been based on superficiality and loneliness. Talking openly to each other, whether to work through the issues or to discover the source of the dissatisfaction, can be a start.

Metaphorical

The goals set out to be accomplished were attained and things have worked out in one's favor. The goal was to complete a program; the program was completed.

GENERAL MEANING FOR 9 OF CUPS

- Things working in your favor, seeking excessive gratification for lack of fulfillment
- A yes card, happy pleasures like sexual expression, narcotics, materialistic
- Satisfaction with work, career, finances; change in plans, trusting someone and not really knowing them

QUESTION STATEMENT:
What makes your relationship satisfying? Dissatisfying?

AFFIRMATION:
I have gratitude and appreciation for all around me.

TIMING:
9 days, 9 weeks, 9 months, September, February 19-March 20

9 of Swords
ASSOCIATED WITH THINKING MIND VS QUIET MIND

3rd Chakra: Yellow color, element of anxiety that leads to growth

Meaning: Thinking obsessively

Location: Solar plexus, abdominal area

When this card is drawn, one finds conversations within one's mind. Everything that one can think of that can go wrong is being thought of – and that is what is causing the worries. What one fears in the relationship is unlikely to manifest in the relationship. However, fear, worry, or doubt still linger in the mind. The sub-conscious thoughts of the situation are being pushed forward to the conscious mind – thoughts like, *what if the worst happens?* surface uncomfortably. The focus is on the negative aspects of an outcome. The fear felt may have developed from the past, causing that past to resurface. The mental resurfacing is fear based, or self-destructive past behavior. There may be physical distance or disconnection between partners and this is what is bringing up the mental anguish. One may be pulling back and not putting enough effort into the relationship, giving the feeling of frustration. The partner may be too wrapped up in daily activities or work, and not paying attention to the needs of the relationship. If one is drawing this card a lot, try doing an activity, like cleaning or exercise, quiet your mind, focus on other senses (like smell or hearing). Do not listen to the negative thoughts within your mind.

Metaphorical

Being blamed for a crime that you did not commit, you were stressed and worried over it, but at the end of the trial you are set free.

GENERAL MEANING FOR 9 OF SWORDS

- Feeling blocked in one's thoughts, people judging you for your situation
- Working towards a goal that is in a competitive area, finances and career going well, having enough money
- Being away from your partner, worries, anxiety, restlessness, impatience all cause lack of sleep

Question Statement:
What are some things that you're currently worried about?
Are they warranted concerns?

Affirmation:
When a fear or thought comes into mind, I know that all will work out in my favor.

Timing:
9 days, 9 weeks, 9 months, September, May 21-June 21

9 of Wands
ASSOCIATED WITH HIDDEN VS EXHIBITED

3rd Chakra: Yellow color, element of confidence

Meaning: Sexual urges

Location: Solar plexus, abdominal area

This card indicates how one expresses personal emotions when relating to certain issues or topics that were repressed/expressed (like sexuality or cultural rules) when growing up, that now come to the surface in the relationship. When a person grows up in a repressed environment, then moves out into the open, they are able to express and explore new things, adding to their character and self-esteem. Issues from the past resurface due to one's personal desire. You may have a partner who loves receiving attention, whether it's from a profession or their own charming personality. Understanding your partner's personality will allow you to see their insecurities and why they seek desires from the past, which may be causing current issues. The partner may be in denial about these issues or may be unaware of their actions relating to them. This may make one feel selfish and unaware when considering how hurtful the actions are to the other. Partners may be making the same mistakes they made in a prior relationship. One who loves the exploration and the idea of having different and multiple partners sexually may fulfill an emotional void that was developed in childhood. The partner may have gotten into the relationship for obligation purposes and now have back-and-forth feelings about staying.

METAPHORICAL

One may be going fishing at sea, but when faced with the duty of catching the fish, they are indecisive about wanting to carry out the act.

GENERAL MEANING FOR 9 OF WANDS

- Waiting for an answer
- Work and income are good
- Flirtatious behavior among co-workers
- Not sure about wanting a commitment in romance

QUESTION STATEMENT:
What past issues are you and your partner arguing about?

AFFIRMATION:
I learn from past experiences and know they help me become a stronger person.

TIMING:
9 days, 9 weeks, 9 months, September, November 22-December 21

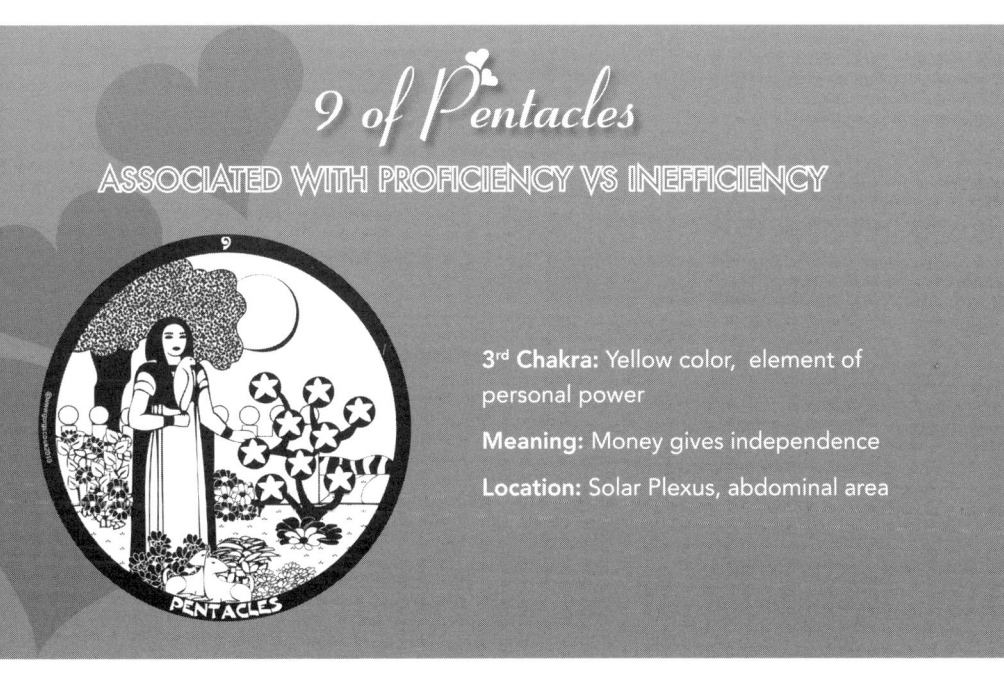

9 of Pentacles
ASSOCIATED WITH PROFICIENCY VS INEFFICIENCY

3rd Chakra: Yellow color, element of personal power

Meaning: Money gives independence

Location: Solar Plexus, abdominal area

One knows the value of their relationship and what it means to them; it has a natural feeling of self-worth and confidence. In a relationship, one likes to be with their partner and interact in social gatherings, but also values time to themselves. If living together, they would like to have their own room (like an office or gym). This person enjoys being in the relationship because they like what their partner gives them, i.e., financial independence, or they like sharing financial success. This is a partner who likes quality items, whether it's designer merchandise or a comfortable lifestyle. They are mature and do not need acceptance from peers for approval of their relationship. Both partners can be critical of each other, but this is an attempt to improve what they feel needs to be improved. There is little emotional expression in public, but between the couple, they let loose. The partner is reliable, trustworthy. A car or some type of transportation may have a significant part in the relationship temporarily. One partner may not take the responsibility for something because he or she relies on what the other has to offer.

METAPHORICAL

Because an extra bonus was in your pay check, you know this will mean that you can buy more than the budget originally allowed. You can splurge and have more of an independence in shopping.

GENERAL MEANING FOR 9 OF PENTACLES

- Animal rights activist, moving to a nicer house or location
- Animal lovers, cats, dogs, outdoors, people who like to shop, busy working, finances increase
- Living arrangement, your hidden desires surface through unexpected actions

QUESTION STATEMENT:
Does your relationship give you the independence you desire?

AFFIRMATION:
Life brings me opportunities to be financially independent.

TIMING:

10 of Cups
ASSOCIATED WITH INVOLVEMENT VS WAVERING

1st Chakra: Color red, element of stability

Meaning: Family unit/structure, sense of responsibility goes to kids and family

Location: Base of the spine area

9 days, 9 weeks, 9 months, September, August 23-September 22

Looking at how one's family structure as a child and adolescent was has an impact on how one behaves in their own relationship. Who is the older, younger, or middle child in their immediate family? There is the bossy firstborn, the romantic middle child, and the friendly last born. Also, coming from a home of divorce or experiencing the death of a parent at an early age can have one partner showing emotional and compatibility issues – are they trying to create disconnect in their relationship or are they emotionally detached? The relationship is supported by family members and shares similar family values and moral, ethical views. It meets a satisfaction level. There may be some disconnect in your relationship, but this has to do with one's dissatisfaction with a career level. One may have a lot of siblings, growing up in a large family. There is a good understanding of the family unit, like how to put daily, routine tasks in order. You both support each other's employment choices. Both have an idea of when things don't feel right in the relationship and what the problem may be. There is good affinity between partners.

METAPHORICAL

Growing up with siblings, each person has different characteristic within their personalities and each relates to one another in a different way.

GENERAL MEANING FOR 10 OF CUPS

- Marriage, ability to agree with openness, celebration
- Family, having a boy first, going on a picnic
- Vacation, career opportunity working with a large corporation

QUESTION STATEMENT:
What character do you play in the relationship?

AFFIRMATION:
I'm self-conscious in what my personality says about me.

TIMING:
10 hours, 10 weeks, 10 months, direction of north, October, February 19-March 20

10 of Swords
ASSOCIATED WITH THOUGHTS VS ACTION

1st Chakra: Color red, element of anew

Meaning: Subconscious mind, negative and positive thinking, external goal versus internal goal

Location: Base of the spine area

    This card depicts that your surface or external relationship isn't matching the way you feel emotionally about the relationship. What you feel inside about you or your partner isn't moving towards your internal goal for the relationship. You or your partner may want to get married (internal goal) but, one isn't taking the necessary actions (external goal), such as making the relationship a committed partnership. The restrictions stem from the mental thought process in how you or your partner view relationships. There may be difficulty expressing or communicating what you want or need. There is a lack of emotional or physical connection causing hindrance in relationship growth. One would like to change the relationship, but he or she is not changing the way they speak, listen, or treat the relationship. They are unaware of sabotaging it out of fear and repeating destructive behavioral patterns, such as arguing, lying, or yelling. Thinking positive thoughts helps with health. This can aid in lowering depression or lessen stress on the stomach. Throughout the day, be aware of your thought patterns and how you can control negative thoughts, turning them into positive ones. Don't let your emotions define your position in the situation; for example, thinking *I feel overwhelmed and stressed, so I have doubts in my ability*, labeling, playing the blame game (like if one gets a flat tire, they blame themselves for the car's break down or labeling oneself a loser or failure).

Metaphorical

Thoughts lead to emotions and emotions lead to action. Each thought we have within our conscious thought process leads to an emotion; that emotion then leads one to act upon it based on how it is perceived.

GENERAL MEANING FOR 10 OF SWORDS

- One may be disappointed about a certain outcome, divorce, back stabbing
- A gain or opportunity that will last as long as you want it to, career move, indecision about a partner
- Change for the better after the worse has happened, only control you have is your thoughts

Question statement:
Your thoughts define your day. What are your first thoughts when you wake up?

Affirmation:
I'm a beautiful and loving person and life loves me.

Timing:
10 hours, 10 weeks, 10 months, direction of west, October, May 21-June 21

10 of Wands
ASSOCIATED WITH SAYING YES VS NO

1st Chakra: Color red, element of survival

Meaning: Ambition – gut intuition

Location: Base of the spine area

One has the strength and drive to take on more tasks due to ambition they have had in their daily life recently. An opportunity has come up, like a new job or new opportunities, that gives one the courage and drive to be determined to carry out the pursuit. Look at the "hierarchy of needs" in your life and relationship. Which need has been focused on most? Is it the psychological along with bodily needs – like sleeping, resting, eating, and exercising? Or does it focus on social needs; relationships with friends, family, and partner; self-esteem fulfillment; achieving a certain desired goal to improve your social status? The relationship has been through different types of obstacles and now you are able to push forward from all the lessons learned from ex relationships as well as the current relationship. This enables the partnership to move in an improved direction. Making plans is needed to allow your ideas to come alive. In verbal communication, you may find how your partner communicates burdensome, like wanting to be mothered in the relationship. Also, when you're busy at work, your partner may be doing something behind your back. One has a strong self-esteem to have the internal strength to want more by working harder. Self-esteem equals ambition. Low self-esteem correlates to creating low ambition, and high self-esteem leads to high ambition.

METAPHORICAL

Coming home from grocery shopping and carrying all the grocery bags inside your home by yourself, the stress and strain on the back is felt, but the feeling of accomplishment is satisfaction is evident.

GENERAL MEANING FOR 10 OF WANDS

- Someone deceitful is around your circle, a divorce that involves kids, desire for a better lifestyle
- Feeling burdened or weighed down by mental or physical tasks, travel for new housing, back discomfort
- Getting a job offer/promotion, making things work because of past learning experiences/difficulties

QUESTION STATEMENT:
What drives your ambitions in life?
Is it family life? Is it career life?
How do you balance them?

AFFIRMATION:
I think consciously about how to balance my priorities.

TIMING:
10 hours, 10 weeks, 10 months, east direction, November 22-December 22

10 of Pentacles
ASSOCIATED WITH SOLE VS ACCOMPANIED

1st Chakra: Color red, element of social order

Meaning: Build positive ego

Location: Base of the spine area

This card indicates looking at one's ego and how that has an effect on the relationship. Equality and respecting one's achievements in the relationship is important. Does one partner try to control the other's decisions or is there freedom in what choices they make? Accept each other for who they are and refrain from listening to your inner critic. It may also represent family legacy, strong family life, and inflexible ideas in how the family organization or unity is conducted (what is accepted or unacceptable). One may be feeling left out, not sharing the same ideology in how daily activities should be implemented.

METAPHORICAL

Sharing the same craft/job as your grandparent and parent is a legacy. Your grandparent was a store owner, followed by your parent, and now you own the store.

GENERAL MEANING FOR 10 OF PENTACLES

- Gaining an inheritance, visiting family, job promotion
- Conscious of good and bad choices, family-owned business, salary increase
- Ego-driven actions, parental influence, not letting outsiders in

QUESTION STATEMENT:
What part of your ego shows up in your relationships?

AFFIRMATION:
I'm open, non-judgmental, and treat people with respect.

TIMING:
10 hours, 10 weeks, 10 months, direction of south, October, August 23-September 22

Chapter 5
The Royalty Cards

Queen of Cups
SCORPIO PERSONALITY

The archetype of this woman is someone who is very intuitive and perceives her information through her senses. She can be a wife, girlfriend, relative, or co-worker archetype. She makes a great homemaker and mother. She easily says *yes* when she means *no*, and more of *yes* than *no* when someone asks her for assistance – and that can create a health hazard for her. Having a balanced self-caring for one's self is important to remember. One's partner can become easily jealous over the littlest things. This can be due to one feeling very secure in the relationship, whereas the other partner may feel less secure. This can be because of their personality or a psychological wound that stems from the past. Wounds can include feeling abandonment as a child – whether it was from abuse, divorce, or just not being heard. So they project what they're feeling onto their partner, creating the same emotions as their own internal ones. As time goes on, one will learn more about their partner, as their self-guard softens. This card can represent a partner who is devoted or one that is moody and likes gossip, but can be fair with encouraging words in times of need. One can be slightly narrow-minded and will never forget who has wronged them.

Metaphorical

Feeling the soft soothing water on the feet when strolling along the beach shore is enjoyable. As the tide changes, the debris from the ocean comes on the shore as well – this changes the feeling of the stroll along the shore.

GENERAL MEANING FOR QUEEN OF CUPS

- Uncontrolled emotions that lead to self-sabotaging behavior, a good animal communicator
- Pay attention to your intuition, dreams, gut feelings, a generous person with money
- A situation that requires more compassion, a secret will be told due to an event that will take place

Question statement:
When was the last time you did a kind act.?

Affirmation:
Everything I do has value.

Timing:
Scorpio, October 23-November 21, Cancer

Queen of Swords
VIRGO PERSONALITY

This card can depict a type of woman around your relationship, like a mother or mother-in-law figure. She can also be a wife, girlfriend, relative, or co-worker Archetype. She is a quick thinker, sharp with her words, and it's hard to put things over on her. In a romantic relationship, this can indicate that the interactions between the partners are cool and somewhat detached. The couple may be living together, but there is no emphasis on any emotional connection. The couple goes on with their daily lives independently, even though they have each other. There are no expressions of excitement with one another; for example, no joking, laughing, or playing around. This can be a phase, or part of one's personality. For a phase, one can be going through a difficult time in life, whether it's a death of someone or difficulty in career. The way that person reacts and deals with the situation is by internalizing and withholding emotion. When the person doesn't know how to deal with their circumstances, it causes them to shut down. Difficulty brings strength; past strife gives strength.

METAPHORICAL

When one defines themselves, or defines another person, using a job as an identity, this does not take into account the way he or she is as a person.

GENERAL MEANING FOR QUEEN OF SWORDS

- Divorce or a widow, a person who uses sarcasm to hide fear
- A narrow mind that leads to emotional manipulation, someone who is very keen to their surroundings
- A woman who is a teacher, or principal, someone feeling alone in how they feel, independence
- Making the right decision in a situation, a decision that is fair and balanced

QUESTION STATEMENT:
A person's job doesn't define who they are as a person.
What's your view on this statement?

AFFIRMATION:
I have faith in the now and the future.

TIMING:
Libra and Virgo, August 23-September 22

Queen of Wands
LEO PERSONALITY

Behavior from the past can hinder your relationship. She can be a wife, girlfriend, relative, or co-worker Archetype. There is great energy between you and your partner; however, one of you keeps bringing up things from the past and won't let it go – this still causes arguments. There may be some deep-seeded resentment regarding what took place in the past, and this fuels the frustration of old baggage. Or, you or your partner may have had issues within a past relationship and now this is being carried forth into this relationship. This card supports a loving partner and person who like to be at home cooking and cleaning, but also has a career. It depicts a person who loves pets, an animal lover, and one who makes them part of the family. Or it can indicate you or your partner's behavior towards one another. Exercising independency of thought in the relationship helps create healthy boundaries; however, when one interferes and tries to control and manipulate their partner, boundaries are broken and this creates resentment from the other half.

METAPHORICAL

It's exciting going on vacation and to a new place, but bringing old clothes and luggage is no fun – dressing in old clothes doesn't support the new trip. When one brings old luggage, it puts stress on the current partner who has to deal with that baggage.

GENERAL MEANING FOR QUEEN OF WANDS

- Someone who dwells on hang ups, new ideas that can formulate into a new career
- Someone with a temper and fails to listen to other people's opinions, good news with a career
- Someone who has unstable emotions that leads to infidelity, increase in work

QUESTION STATEMENT:
Is there any interference in the relationship?

AFFIRMATION:
I can't control another; I can only control what I accept and do.

TIMING:
Leo, July 23-August 22

Queen of Pentacles
AQUARIUS PERSONALITY

The archetype in this card depicts a serious and hardworking woman with little fooling around. She can be a wife, girlfriend, relative, or co-worker archetype. In a relationship, this can indicate that your finances and career direction is doing well, but romantically, there can be a need for more laughing and joking, or spontaneous moments that allow for someone to be vulnerable with their surface emotions. Not only does laughing make one feel good, but there are numerous benefits. Some of them are:

- The reduction of stressful emotions, like pain and anxiety
- An increase in the immune system
- An increase in the release of endorphins, which increase the feeling of wellness

Your partner may be focused on too much judging or criticizing regarding where one is in life and not meeting up to these expectations. Starting with a smile and having you and your partner sit with each other, telling jokes or sharing funny stores, will help open the door to one feeling comfortable in letting down their guard. This may be difficult for one, if they had to grow up fast in their childhood, but with practice, one can improve.

METAPHORICAL

The structure of a firecracker is solid and bright with a lot of colors. When you light it up, the flame displays an array of brightness and intensity from the solid stability of the structure.

GENERAL MEANING FOR QUEEN OF PENTACLES

- Starting a new business or investment, job offer, someone who lacks a sense of humor
- Someone who is sensitive, reliable, and practical, great time for conception of birth
- A yes card, any financial transaction with paper work goes good, unexpected events

QUESTION STATEMENT:
When was the last time you had a good laugh?
Did you share it with your partner?

AFFIRMATION:
I love to laugh and joke and share with an open heart.

TIMING:
Aquarius, January 20-February 20

King of Cups
CANCER PERSONALITY

An archetype of a man who is very compassionate towards one's needs, also giving and responsible. This can be a brother, husband, relative, co-worker, or friend. This is a very nurturing relationship, each learning from the other and able to accept their points of view. One is very insightful in the motives of others and is very intuitive. When you and your partner argue, your partner never forgets when you wronged them and may hold resentment that is not spoken about, but will show in retaliation later. Expression of emotions, like crying and laughing, are seen in the relationship, whether it's when watching a sad or funny movie, listening to a song, or reading a book. The ability to be in touch with one's emotions allows for inner intuition to be heightened. Expressing an emotional response like crying is a healthy thing because the partner is allowing him or herself to feel and to be vulnerable at that moment. This card has nothing to do with the attachment theory, where one leaves and the other cries. Crying allows those emotions felt to be expressed, whether from something sad or happy, and releases endorphins and reduces blood pressure. The ability for one to be in touch with one's emotions enables that person to have compassion and moral and ethical views. When boundaries are broken continuously with a person who is in touch with their emotions, they can lash out in a spiteful manner and react in ways that are not of characteristic of them.

Metaphorical

Watching a romantic movie that moves you to tears with the compelling story that is told can reach the depths of one's empathic soul. It allows you to really feel what one is going through in the story plot.

GENERAL MEANING FOR KING OF CUPS

- Emotional man who has wondering eyes, business deals go well
- Profession that involves science and medicine, owning your own business
- A passionate professor, doctor, or priest; a move is possible due to new direction
- A good husband, son, brother, employee; scandal that resulted out of a love affair

Question statement:
When was the last time you saw your partner cry?

Affirmation:
When I cry, I let out my anxiety and bring in my happiness.

Timing:
Scorpio, Cancer, June 21-July 22

King of Swords
LIBRA PERSONALITY

The archetype pattern is someone who doesn't express their emotions; he thinks more with his analytical mind than with a compassionate heart. This can be a brother, husband, co-worker, relative, or friend. In the relationship, it may feel that your partner isn't listening to you, your needs, or concerns, and you may take it as them ignoring the situation. In fact, that is not the case. It's just the way they are; one may find it hard to get a response or a sense of direction from them. Backing off and focusing on what one has to do for themselves, is one way to deal with this situation. Eventually, the partner comes around and things are discussed. This situation really puts a partner's patience to the test.

METAPHORICAL

When it's been snowing outside all day, and you get into your car to start it and warm it up, it needs to run for a few minutes before it begins to warm up inside. Everyone has a different personality – some quiet, loud, or shy. Understanding what type of personality your partner has enables more of a continuity in a relationship.

GENERAL MEANING FOR KING OF SWORDS

- Surgeons, an ex who causes inference for selflessness
- Someone ambitious, questionable intentions, concern about work or career
- A person who is insecure and hides it through educational talk, money is made under tension
- Obstacles experienced when traveling

Question statement:
Do you feel like it takes time for your partner to respond to you when you ask them a question?

Affirmation:
I don't allow other people's responses to affect me.

Timing:
Aquarius, January 19-February 18

King of Wands
ARIES PERSONALITY

Impulsive, ambitious, and independent are the Archetype themes in this card; it can represent a father, husband, relative, friend, or co-worker. In the relationship, compassion and kind feelings are expressed. The relationship is based on having things in order, such as, tax returns are filed at the appropriate time, bills are paid on time, and appointments are kept. So there is a pretty good flow. If the couple is going through a rough patch, solutions at this time are given easily. One may be more demanding in what solutions to go with – each has their own idea about how to solve issues – so respecting each other's boundaries is important. Talking and writing down the different types of solutions to problems facing the relationship can be a creative process. You or your partner may have a temper that is controlled. One may suppress their feelings and emotions, then erupt into anger because of the inability to express their feelings; the upset and frustration builds up until it explodes. This may become a surprise to you or your partner when it occurs, but talking about it will help the relationship.

METAPHORICAL

Having a schedule allows one to prioritize what needs to be addressed first and what is to come later. Writing down goals each day helps achieve those goals and makes things attainable. The more specific one is, the more focus in there is for the desired accomplishment.

GENERAL MEANING FOR KING OF WANDS

- Work increases at this time; an educated, married person
- Job offers, expressing opinions can lead to arguments
- Invitation to travel, passionate time

QUESTION STATEMENT:
Do you feel like your relationship reads like a schedule?

AFFIRMATION:
I decide when to give up, not other people.

TIMING:
Leo, July 22-August 22

King of Pentacles
GEMINI PERSONALITY

The Archetype for this card is a man who stands for his beliefs, tend to be emotionless and somewhat insensitive to other people's needs. This can represent a father figure, husband, friend, relative, or co-worker. In relationships, this card shows an urgency to be more attentive towards one's emotional needs. When someone is unable, or doesn't know how, to express feelings or needs in the relationship, they project that hidden issue onto something else to fill that void. This could include working a lot, focusing on making money or breaking boundary behaviors (cheating). Just as one is stingy with expressing their feelings, they can be this same way with their money. Focus on financial issues and career takes center stage; however, when intimacy comes in, the partner only expresses their desires at that moment. The rest of the time, they are without expressions of surface intimacy. The partner needs to realize that there is more than just that "bed intimacy." There is everyday communication, affection intimacy. Whether it's scratching their partner's back, hugging, or kissing. There is a need to change the past behavioral pattern to have a new outcome.

METAPHORICAL

Pillows, bed sheets, and bedspreads are all components of what makes up a comforting bed. Sharing a bed with a rock as a partner does not reciprocate any emotional warmth.

GENERAL MEANING FOR KING OF PENTACLES

- Job offer that leads to a promotion, takes time to make a decision
- A clever person, financial stability, money in the bank, commitment, dull
- Good in building, math, and teaching; sneaky, cheats; down-to-earth, hard working, reliable

QUESTION STATEMENT:
Do you feel you have enough affection in the relationship?

AFFIRMATION:
I'm thankful that when I give my word; I keep it.

TIMING:
Taurus, April 21-April 21

Chapter 6
Court of the Knights

Knight of Cups
PISCES ENERGY

The Knight of Cups is an archetype of a (30 to 40s) male or female. You may be attracted to a person who is not interested in being involved in a committed relationship. However, the partner represents physically what you desire in a partner. Wrapped up into your dreams, are you seeing your partner in the way the situation really is? You and your partner are very warm and charming, and you feel a strong connection – like this may be the one. What you're envisioning in your relationship can take time to develop; the idea of idealism is what drives this relationship. Your feelings, thoughts, and the way you're perceiving how the relationship moves forward is hindering what is actually manifesting. Your partner may be questioning if the relationship is practical for their life. Work on what is present now and this will give you the knowledge to move forward. There needs to be boundaries within one's self, and a knowledge about what a relationship means and what is healthy growth and acceptable. Being in a relationship with someone already married doesn't allow you to glean your full potential. Someone can be sensitive to their partner's needs and stay in a relationship, and can still wonder off to infidelity. Infidelity is co-created; the person who is refusing to face the facts and the other person refusing to listen. This is someone who loves to be in love, but doesn't commit because they have the fear of getting hurt. They end up cheating or breaking up with their partner instead of working on the problem.

Metaphorical

Buying an item based on the outward appearance is eye catching. An example might be a car – it has all the interior design that one wanted, but when driving it, it's not comfortable.

GENERAL MEANING FOR KNIGHT OF CUPS

- A compassionate and gentle person, someone advancing at work, uncontrolled emotions
- Listen to your intuition, the woman or man of your dreams, being invited to an event
- Attraction that came as a surprise, going away to school, unexpected financial gain

Question Statement:
Is there any social pressure around you or your relationship – like when to have kids? Marriage?

Affirmation:
Other people's views or comments don't upset me.

Timing:
2 days, or 2 months, or the month of February

Knight of Swords
GEMINI ENERGY

The Knight of Swords is an Archetype of a (30 to 40s) male or female. Quick action is happening: a *yes* card for a question asked, a situation that is able to bring people together and formulate work. Your partner may be easily bored and impatient with you at times, and they may get upset because you're not "acting as fast as they are." One may be focused on immediate gratification in the relationship, due to them feeling restless. Money may be an issue regarding how it is spent and who is spending it irresponsibly. When problems arise in the relationship, the emotions behind the problem are not addressed, such as how one is feeling about the situation – are they fearful? Concerned? Happy, or unhappy? Instead, the solution is focused on what steps are needed to make that necessary change. The communication in the relationship is not two sided; in fact, one partner is doing more of the talking then the other. It's good to be flexible with your partner and conduct regular check ins with each other, such as discussion about finances (spending what and when), or how impulsive actions affect the other person in the relationship (creating anxiety and untrusted feelings). We have no control of other people; we have control only of ourselves and what *we* are ready to accept as healthy, thus enabling us to grow in the relationship.

METAPHORICAL

When unexpected opportunities come up (i.e., a job or relationship), it brings excitement and change that requires choices to be made. You suddenly get that job promotion; now you're happy, but a new change also comes with that opportunity.

GENERAL MEANING FOR KNIGHT OF SWORDS

- Someone making impulsive choices or actions, someone that likes to talk and is easily distracted
- Straightforward, inconsistent actions, a situation or event that will make you feel stimulated
- Unexpected directions, someone who spends money and doesn't save, a feeling of freedom

Question Statement:
Does your partner help you when you need assistance?
Do you trust their input?

Affirmation:
I visualize my success.

Timing:
6 days, or 6 months, or the month of June

Knight of Wands
SAGITTARIUS ENERGY

The Knight of Wands is an Archetype of a (30 to 40s) male or female. This card is about travel and a need for a plan to show where the relationship is going. Where do you see you and your partner in one, two, three years? Not having an idea or goals that lead to plans create an oppressive feel to the relationship. You and your partner get along well, but there may be things that need to be worked out to keep the relationship moving. The plan is like a blueprint to build your home; your home is the relationship between you and your partner. Also, you or your partner may travel for work, or relocate for work; both of you are willing to work at the relationship. Is one trying to be the rescuer, trying to make plans for the future because of a lack of trying from the other partner? This can cause the person who is trying to do the rescuing to forget about what needs to be planned for in their own life, which can be a self-abandonment issue. One may see the way the relationship should be headed, and the other partner may not see it just yet.

METAPHORICAL

When building a home, the blueprint of the architecture of the house needs to be drawn up first to start the building process. The contractors start with the layout and house dimensions for the success of the building.

GENERAL MEANING FOR KNIGHT OF WANDS

- Being in a long distance relationship, a sudden opportunity that leads to unexpected gains
- Moving for a job, relocation, spontaneous actions or events, troublemaker, clear vision
- Changing jobs, careers, homes; change in the relationship due to changes in one's career

Question Statement:
Where is your relationship headed in the next year? Two years?

Affirmation:
I'm open to other solutions to my problems.

Timing:
11 days, or 11 months, or the month of November

Knight of Pentacles
VIRGO ENERGY

The Knight of Pentacles is an Archetype of a (30 to 40s) male or female. In a relationship, there is slow and steady growth – both emotional and financial. There will be an increase in the growth of the relationship, and the mobility to move forward through the problems you're facing. In the past, you, your partner, or both of you have made changes to some behavioral patterns – listening more, being more open to communication and feelings – enabling you to allow the relationship to move forward towards a more fixed goal for a successful life. This also can reflect that you or your partner know what is wanted from life and have a strong idea in knowing how to get there. One or both partners are reliable and focused on what they want to achieve. This card also represents a person who likes to travel; you or your partner may have been to, or lived in, different places.

METAPHORICAL

Working out and counting the calorie intake daily allows one to lose weight. Each week, one can lose one to two pounds; within six months, forty pounds could be lost with consistency of growth.

GENERAL MEANING FOR KNIGHT OF PENTACLES

- A person that is reliable, a good time for any scholastic endeavors
- Slow business transactions that reach a successful outcome, someone likes gardening
- Someone who hides their feelings/emotions, health and fitness
- New opportunities, a good source of income, property, real estate sells

Question statement:
Do you feel like your relationship has a sense of direction?

Affirmation:
Patience allows me to embrace the important things in life.

Timing:
9 days, or 9 months, or the month of September

Chapter 7
Court of Pages

Page of Cups
WATER SIGN

The Page of Cups is an Archetype of a (20 to 30s) male or female. Having healthy emotional boundaries allow each partner to have separate thoughts and feelings. This card indicates one who should take responsibility for his or her own feelings and not blame the other partner for the way they feel. Your partner is secure in who they are and not focusing every emotion or event on how that impacts you; there is the ability to share. An innovated partner, this card depicts someone stopping the forward movement due to an immature display of emotions. Someone from the past may be trying to cause problems with emotional interference.

METAPHORICAL

When a person is emotionally immature and becomes mad at the other person, they lash out in gossip and make up fake stories about that person.

GENERAL MEANING FOR PAGE OF CUPS

- Use your intuition, traveling, job opportunity
- Mother's favorite, relationship causes distraction
- Gossip/lies due to immaturity and an insecure person, good financial standing

QUESTION STATEMENT:
How would you define your emotional boundaries?
Are they strong or do they need improvement?

AFFIRMATION:
I ignore any negative talk.

TIMING:
Within one week

Page of Swords
AIR SIGN

The Page of Swords is an Archetype of a (20 to 30s) male or female. This card indicates someone who is quick, clever, and able to do something behind a partner's back. The person may not be addressing issues because they haven't experienced them before or they believe a partner wouldn't act in a certain way. When this card shows, you or your partner are not paying attention to actions. This may be due to the niceness that one or the other think is present in the relationship. There may be a feeling of stability, but actions that are taking place are not being voiced openly. You or your partner may have never experienced what is going on now. So things can be done, literally, behind you or your partner's back. Or there may be a situation where you or your partner have a lack of information, so this gives partners ways of involving deceiving actions. Things are happening quickly in your relationship. It may lead you to have a feeling of insecurity – that may be the underlying issue of you or your partner's actions.

METAPHORICAL

Finances are a big part of a relationship. When someone else knows the account number to another's banking and does not check the statements, this leaves money vulnerable for misuse of funds. The person with the bank account would never think that this would happen, because they've never experienced it, nor have they been around that type of behavior.

GENERAL MEANING FOR PAGE OF SWORDS

- Emotional interface with work, having the ability to deal with problems that arise
- A person acting like a friend, but is in fact a double dealer; read all the fine print when signing papers
- Unexpected occurrence that brings about good change, messages, phone calls with good news

Question Statement:
Do you ever have the feeling your partner is doing something behind your back? If so, did you talk about it?

Affirmation:
I enjoy having new opportunities come into my life.

Timing:
Within one week

Page of Wands
FIRE SIGN

The Page of Wands is an Archetype of a (20 to 30s) male or female. This card indicates a person who is passionate in their craft, a school-oriented person, and someone with good intentions. It may feel that your relationship is always on the go, whether it's meetings, social events, or family obligations. There is great excitement when partners are together, but having space is also needed to develop healthy boundaries. One partner may experience anxiety over attachment issues; they like being with their partner and can tend to suffocate them with their overzealous enthusiasm. Attachment issues can stem from their inner child of nurturing. One has a sense of security or closeness when around their mate, but when apart experience separation anxiety. Since the attachment development starts with the way the person was nurtured with their own parents, this has to be talked about to discover how they feel secure and safe. Some signs of attachment problems are: feeling suffocated in a healthy relationship, not trusting a partner, being overly suspicious because of being insecure within one's self, or sex giving the feeling of being taken care of or nurtured.

METAPHORICAL

Going to an event with food, beverages, and entertainment can be a lot of fun. Time goes by fast, enjoying the social company and the complementary delights. When it's time to leave, one may wish it to last longer.

GENERAL MEANING FOR PAGE OF WANDS

- Creative ideas in work, resourceful, a person with good intentions or ideas
- Good news in finances, any type of paper work, hard worker who seeks more out of life
- A situation that needs more time to develop, travel for job opportunity, criticism that brings anger
- Owning your own business, sexual energy, stimulation, attraction

Question statement:
When was the last time you did something fun with your partner?

Affirmation:
I get excited when I see my partner.

Timing:
Within one week

Page of Pentacles
EARTH SIGN

The Page of Pentacles is an Archetype of a grounded, young male or female (20 to 30s), an earth sign, and a faithful lover who can be immature. This one expresses their affection to their partner as conditional love, meaning that if a partner is acting in a desired way, then they will engage in the relationship. This can be because the partner is unaware that they are putting these conditions on the partner, reflecting their own feelings towards that partner. This is also a form of control. Conditional love puts limits and boundaries between partners. It's important to make each other feel appreciated and to keep the relationship front and center. The honeymoon stage with all the excitement and fun has changed; it's important to still have a date night. Relationships have different stages, as each person's feelings change and the relationship progresses. Being aware of this and not taking one for granted gives each partner a realistic view. The partner is able to have unconditional love, once they work through their reasons.

METAPHORICAL

Giving and receiving affection is a natural human process of intimacy, but when a person says that they will give you a hug only if you hug them first, this is conditioning the process.

GENERAL MEANING FOR PAGE OF PENTACLES

- Traveling locally, small business owner, monogamous relationship
- Beginning of a job opportunity, not knowing what action to take with a loved one
- Going to school, learning a new subject, unaware of how their actions affect people

QUESTION STATEMENT:
Have you experienced unconditional love in your relationship?

AFFIRMATION:
I love my partner in my daily thoughts.

TIMING:
Within one week

Conclusion

Reading Tarot cards can be fun and enlightening. Each relationship is a unique learning lesson and Tarot gives you an added insight into the root of the psyche. Pulling daily cards and seeing what issue can be addressed within yourself and your relationship is a private dealing – and tarot is dynamic tool for that. With more than fifteen years conducting relationship readings for people from different backgrounds, I was able to construct this book for the purpose of shedding some light onto the dynamic Tarot language and how it can help one better understand the relationship elements. Whether you're a Tarot professional or a beginner, this book is written for any level of reader. Adding your own experience and input to what is learned in this book adds to your Tarot knowledge.

THANKS FOR READING AND ENJOY!

NOTES